The companion Volume, similarly bound

Abbeys

By M. R. JAMES, Litt.D., F.S.A., F.B.A., Provost of Eton, with an additional chapter on "Monastic Life and Buildings," by A. Hamilton Thompson, M.A., D.Litt., F.S.A., Professor of Mediæval History in the University of Leeds.

With One Hundred Illustrations by Photographic Reproduction, Fifty - Six Drawings, Thirteen Plans, Seven Colour Plates and Map.

May be obtained from any Great Western Station or bookstall or from your bookseller.

PRICE

5/-

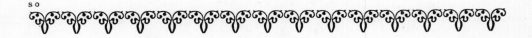

CATHEDRALS

LONDON

SOUTHWARK

WESTMINSTER

CATHEDRALS

WITH SEVENTY-FOUR ILLUSTRATIONS BY PHOTOGRAPHIC REPRODUCTION AND SEVENTY-FOUR DRAWINGS

THE GREAT WESTERN RAILWAY
[FELIX J. C. POLE, GENERAL MANAGER]
PADDINGTON STATION, LONDON

First Edition, March 1924   30,000 *copies*
Second Edition, July 1925   10,000 *copies*

Printed in England on British Paper at THE BALLANTYNE PRESS
SPOTTISWOODE, BALLANTYNE & CO. LTD. Colchester, London, & Eton

Lambeth Palace. S.E

24th January 1924.

My dear Churchill,

I am delighted to see the proof of your forthcoming
Great Western volume.   The way in which it presents to the
public the beauty and character of the great Cathedrals which
stand within your range is beyond praise.   No one can travel
much without being struck by the number of people whom one
meets in a railway carriage who are passing unintelligently
through places of the very foremost historic interest or
natural beauty or architectural glory.   This unintelligence is
due simply to lack of opportunity to know better.   Any
endeavour to promote a truer understanding of the wonders
which your Railway brings within the reach of all of us is
entitled to our warmest welcome and co-operation.   You will be
rendering a wonderful service to the English people and to
visitors from overseas if you will help them to realise better
the sacred heritage which is ours.   Surely this is above all
true when you reproduce for our guidance the beauties of the
great Cathedrals with which your pages deal.

Most cordially do I commend your endeavour and wish
it the uttermost success.

I am, Yours very truly,

Randall Cantuar:

The above is a copy of a letter from His Grace the Archbishop of Canterbury to Viscount
Churchill, Chairman of the Great Western Railway.

v

THE MARCH TO CALVARY: TINWORTH'S TERRACOTTA IN TRURO CATHEDRAL

CONTENTS

AND A SPECIAL MAP
Showing the Cathedrals, Abbeys and Castles
within the area served by the
Great Western Railway
(*see page 3 of cover*)

WESTMINSTER ABBEY: THE NORTH PORCH

WESTMINSTER ABBEY: THE CHAPEL OF HENRY VII

WESTMINSTER ABBEY: THE TOMB OF THE UNKNOWN WARRIOR

WESTMINSTER ABBEY: THE EAST CLOISTER, SHOWING ENTRANCES TO THE
CHAPTER HOUSE AND PYX CHAPEL, WITH THE DARK CLOISTER BEYOND

Facing page 1

WESTMINSTER ABBEY

I T is extremely difficult now to visualise the site of Westminster Abbey as it was in the Second Century, when tradition says the first church was erected there by the mythical Lucius, King of the Britons. In "The Historic Thames" Mr. Hilaire Belloc writes thus of a later period : "The site was typical of all those which the great monasteries of the West were to turn from desert places to gardens ; it was a waste tract of ground called 'Thorney,' lying low, triangular in shape, bounded by the two reedy streams that descended through the depression which now runs across the Green Park and Mayfair, and emptied themselves into the Thames, the one just above, the other 100 or 200 yards below, the site of the Houses of Parliament." One of the two reedy streams was the Tyburn, which flowed from the high ground above Hampstead and, connected with a dyke on the west, formed in the river an island, a little over three-quarters of a mile in circumference, overgrown with brambles and thorns, which earned it the name " Thornea," or " Thorney."

There, according to tradition, a temple of Apollo was destroyed by an earthquake in the time of Antoninus Pius. That Roman buildings did exist on the site of the Abbey, proof is forthcoming from the discoveries of Roman tiles, bricks, portions of pavement, door pivots, etc., beneath the Nave, while a Roman sarcophagus found near by is to be seen by the door of the present Chapter House. Moreover, as Mr. Belloc points out, " a great prehistoric road, that of Watling Street [which stretched from Dover to Chester], is believed to correspond with the line of that very ugly suspension bridge which runs from Lambeth to the Horseferry Road in Westminster." Again, a Westminster Charter gives the Roman name of our latter-day Oxford Street—a short distance from the Abbey—as the " Via Militaris."

If Lucius founded a church on Thorney, then that said to have been built by Sebert, King of the East Angles and nephew of Ethelbert, was the second. Sebert gave his church to " the honour of God and St. Peter," to mark his baptism by Mellitus, Bishop of London.

Around the Saxon church was woven a beautiful legend of St. Peter, " accompanied by angels and surrounded with glorious burning lights," having consecrated the building on the day before that appointed by Sebert. In " The History and Antiquities of Westminster Abbey " it is set forth : " Gervase of Canterbury records that, in accordance with the solicitation of Mellitus, who accompanied St. Augustine on his mission to England and had been appointed Bishop of London, Sebert founded the Abbey " ; whilst others, Ralph de Diceto and William of Malmesbury, give the credit of the foundation solely to Bishop Mellitus. Widmore was inclined to throw doubt on Sebert as founder, contending that the claim was based on charters " of which their being forgeries there is no doubt," and great authorities like Dr. Armitage Robinson, Dean of Westminster before becoming Dean of Wells, have exploded the story.

In the South Ambulatory to-day may be seen the reputed tomb of King Sebert and his Queen, who died in September 615 and July 616 respectively. It was the early custom to bury a founder within the precincts of his own foundation—a fact which is held in some quarters to emphasise the claim that Sebert did establish a church here.

Wulsinus (or Wulsius or Wulfius) is the first abbot to whom historians give any accredited notice. The name " West Minster " first appears in a charter of King Offa of Mercia endowing an already existing monastery (A.D. 785) with certain lands at Aldenham.

Mr. Hilaire Belloc says : " The moment the foundation was established a stream of wealth tended towards it ; it was at the very gate of the largest commercial city in the Kingdom, and it was increasingly associated, as the Anglo-Saxon monarchy developed, with the power of the Central Government." About A.D. 958 King Edgar, at the instance of St. Dunstan, restored Sebert's edifice, and Edward the Confessor made a great donation and rebuilt the Abbey (A.D. 1050–1065). Near the Abbey was the Royal Palace, and to that Palace eventually came the Mother of Parliaments.

Clifford wrote : " Without the walls of London upon the river Thames, there was in times passed a little monastery . . . with a few Benedict monks in it, under an abbot, serving Christ : very poor they were, and little was given them for their relief. Here the King [Edward the Confessor] intended

The Shrine of
Edward the Confessor

to make his sepulchre : he commanded, therefore, that of the tenths of all his rents the work should be begun in such sort as should become the Prince of the Apostles. At his commandment the work was nobly begun. . . . He granted to the church great privileges above all churches in the land."

On " the Twelfth Mass Eve " following the consecration of the Abbey on December 28, 1065, Edward the Confessor died and was buried the next day. " The Church then consecrated," in the opinion of Dr. W. R. Lethaby, the Surveyor of Westminster Abbey, " closely resembled the great abbey church at Jumièges, the finest work of the early Norman school. Westminster is represented, with an attempt at accuracy, on the famous Bayeux embroidery as a Church having a great central tower, above what is inscribed as ' The Church of St. Peter's.' Foundations of the Confessor's Church still exist under the present floor, and their resemblance to the work at Jumièges suggests that a Norman building master must have been employed by the Saxon King. After the Conquest the works were continued, and the existing Dormitory passage was erected about A.D. 1080." In the museum attached to the Abbey may be seen a portion of the cloister, considered to date from A.D. 1100.

In the early half of the Thirteenth Century Henry III began rebuilding the church east of the nave, laying the foundation-stone of the Lady Chapel in 1220. The portion of the present edifice east of the choir screen, which was consecrated A.D. 1269, is the work of that monarch. " The part of the cloister attached to the choir and transept," Dr. Lethaby wrote in the special number of *The Times* issued on June 29, 1920, in connection with Dean Ryle's appeal for funds (in a year over £164,000 was raised, donations were world-wide) to restore the Abbey, " belongs to Henry's work, as does also the noble octagonal Chapter House. . . . The work shows knowledge of Amiens and the Ste. Chapelle, as well as of Reims. The forms of the piers and arches and the profiles of mouldings, all the points that would be settled by the building master, are traditionally English. French influence is everywhere, but of direct French invention, authentic and immediate, I cannot find a trace. Either the master mason was trained in the English school or he had worked there long enough to forget the French style-accent. . . . The interior of the Church still preserves more of its old features and furnishings than almost any of our cathedrals. . . . The Abbey Church is the chief and central work of our English art, and a great storehouse of mediæval sculpture and painting. . . . The serious study of our national arts must begin at the Abbey."

Henry's work—which he pursued with passionate interest, born of a deep reverence for the Confessor, employing first Henry, then John of Gloucester, and afterwards Richard of Beverley as master masons, and even those skilled in the intricacies of the art of mosaic from the guilds of Rome—was neglected by Edward I, who found that the building had been carried as far as the first bay beyond the screen on which the organ now stands. During subsequent reigns little was done to the Abbey until Richard II and then Henry V took up the trust, and, writes the Rev. Canon H. F. Westlake, F.S.A., Custodian of the Abbey, " with many vicissitudes, the work was carried on with that conservatism in the matter of style which adds a unity and harmony which largely contribute to its special beauty." The later Abbots, more particularly Estney and Islip, made a great effort to complete it, and, if we except the un-fortunate addition of Hawksmoor's western towers (after a modification of designs by Wren in 1714), the work may be said to have ended with an entry made in the early months of the year 1536 :

> Item for paynted peecis sett in to the west
>   wyndowe and some of coloryd glass
>   in other wyndowes . . . . . . XVJd.

The Abbey stands, with the sole exception of Salisbury Cathedral, as the most perfect example in Pointed Style of architecture in this country. It is, moreover, the " most unique and priceless treasure " of our race—a great heritage from our Anglo-Saxon progenitors. It is the most widely celebrated church in the British Empire, occupying at the same time a position without parallel amongst the ecclesiastical edifices of the world. Here before the High Altar all the sovereigns, excepting Edward V, have been crowned from Harold, the last of the Saxon monarchs, and William the Conqueror, to our august sovereign King George V. Here is the Coronation Chair with the Scone stone, or Stone of Destiny, on which Celtic Kings were crowned : in that chair every British sovereign since Edward I has been crowned, and Cromwell was seated in it when he was proclaimed Protector, for which ceremony the chair was taken into Westminster Hall. The Abbey also has been the burying-place of many of the more celebrated Kings and Queens of England, from Edward the Confessor onwards to George II.

The Coronation Chair
with the Stone of Scone beneath

Near the tomb of Henry III are those of Edward I and his consort Eleanor. Edward ordered that 100 waxlights " should burn for ever around her tomb on St. Andrew's Eve," and provided an endowment for that purpose. Each Abbot of Westminster, it is said, on taking office, was bound by oath to observe this injunction. On the south side lie Edward III and Queen Philippa, Richard II—whose reign brought great prosperity to the Monastery—and Anne of Bohemia. Eastwards lies Henry V, whose exquisite chantry speaks to his memory. Of the Lady Chapel—better known as King Henry VII's Chapel, containing the wonderful tomb and effigies of the monarch and his wife—one cannot do better than recall the words of Washington Irving :

" I stood before the entrance to Henry the Seventh's chapel. A flight of steps led up to it, through a deep and gloomy, but magnificent arch. Great gates of brass, richly and delicately wrought, turn heavily upon their hinges, as if reluctant to admit the feet of common mortals into this most gorgeous of sepulchres. On entering the eye is astonished by the pomp of architecture, and the elaborate beauty of sculptured detail. The very walls are wrought into universal ornament, incrusted with tracery, and scooped into niches, crowded with the statues of Saints and Martyrs. Stone seems by the cunning labour of chisel to have been robbed of its weight and density, suspended aloft as if by magic, and the fretted work achieved with the wonderful minuteness and airy security of a cobweb. Along the sides of the chapel are the lofty stalls of the Knights of the Bath. . . ."

In this Chapel and its aisles are the graves of Edward VI, Queen Mary, Queen Bess, Mary Queen of Scots, Charles II, William and Mary, Queen

4

Anne, and George II. The tombs and memorials in other parts of the Abbey to the illustrious dead are an epitome of the history of our Empire. There are statesmen—Chatham, Pitt, Fox, George and Charles Canning, Palmerston, Gladstone, Beaconsfield, Salisbury, Campbell-Bannerman, and Bonar Law ; philanthropists—Wilberforce, Livingstone, Shaftesbury ; inventors and men of science—Newton, Herschel, Darwin, Watt, Stephenson, Lyell, Hooker, Kelvin, and Lister ; poets and dramatists—Chaucer, Spenser, Southey, Wordsworth, Cowley, Shakespeare, Ben Jonson, Milton, Dryden, Gray, Burns, Isaac Watts, Longfellow, Tennyson, and Browning ; men of letters—Addison, Oliver Goldsmith, Grote, Thackeray, Johnson, Macaulay, Sir Walter Scott, Charles Dickens, and Ruskin ; music is represented by Handel, Balfe, and Jenny Lind ; the theatre by Garrick and Irving ; Clive, Wolfe, Warren Hastings, Lord Lawrence, Lord Strathcona, and Lord Cromer were Empire builders. These are but a few of the many names collated. In the centre of the Nave is undoubtedly the greatest of all tributes—that to " The Unknown Warrior "—the memorial of our reverence for the great and glorious British dead who sacrificed all for the honour of Country and Empire in the Great War. No more fitting resting-place, no more honoured spot could have been chosen for the Nation's tribute to its sons and daughters than this.

That Westminster should have become the burying-place for the greatest of these realms is no doubt due to the reverence attaching to the memory of the Confessor, to whose name the Norman kings were ready to do honour.

When the monastery of St. Peter's was dissolved in A.D. 1540, on the surrender of the revenues Henry VIII raised the status of Westminster to that of a city, and gave it a Bishop, whose diocese embraced Middlesex, with the exception of Fulham. Only one prelate, Thomas Thurleby, held the office, for in 1550 the new see was suppressed and Thurleby translated to Norwich. From then until 1556 the Abbey became part of the See of London. In the latter year Mary revived monasticism and appointed Feckenham as Abbot. He was replaced by a Dean (William Bill) with twelve prebendaries, by Queen Elizabeth, who never abated her interest in the Collegiate Church of St. Peter's at Westminster and the School.

Queen Bess granted the whole property of the Abbey, not only the whole site, but all the chapels to the Dean and Chapter of her new foundation.

Visitors from the United States of America will find in the Abbey many links with Great Britain. Near the Chapter House is the

The Elizabeth Nightingale Monument

memorial window to James Russel Lowell, poet, essayist and U.S. minister to the Court of St. James's from 1880 to 1885, a period just prior to the elevation of the United States Legation to the position of an Embassy. Lowell materially influenced the improvement between the two great English-speaking nations. Poet's Corner contains the remains of Richard Hakluyt, who chronicled the voyages of the early navigators to the western lands across the Atlantic. There is also a fine bust of Longfellow. Near William Congreve's tomb in the Nave is the grave of George Peabody, the American philanthropist. In the south Aisle are the remains of Major John André (d. 1780), and the monument erected by George III depicting André petitioning Washington.

The Abbey is cruciform in shape, with two western towers and a central tower, which is only a few feet higher than the roof. The length of the exterior of the building is 531 feet; that of the transepts is 203 feet; and the Nave is, without the aisles, 38 feet 7 inches wide and 102 feet high. The structure consists of a nave with aisles (in the south transept the eastern cloister walk takes the place of the western aisle), choir, six chapels, and the eastern Lady Chapel (Henry VIIth's Chapel). The celebrated effigies in wax which were, according to custom, carried in funeral processions until 1735, are to be seen in Abbot Islip's Chapel. The Cloisters are thirteenth- and fourteenth-century work. In the eastern cloister is the Norman Chapel of the Pyx, with its altar *in situ*, which was part of the subvault of the original dormitory. It is the oldest remaining part of the Abbey, reaching back to the period of Edward the Confessor's building. In this chapel were kept at one time the standard coins of the realm used in the Trial of the Pyx, and it was the Treasury for the Exchequer. From the same cloister is reached the Chapter House, built in A.D. 1250, and used, together with the Refectory, from A.D. 1282 to A.D. 1547 for the meetings of the House of Commons, which were subsequently appointed to take place in St. Stephen's Chapel of Westminster Palace. The

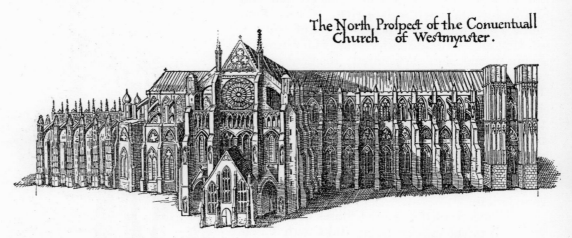

The North Prospect of the Conuentuall Church of Westmynster.

The Abbey Church as left at the Dissolution of the Monastery in 1540

Chapter House has a finely executed tiled floor, laid down in A.D. 1265, and some interesting remains of late fourteenth-century paintings. The Jerusalem Chamber, part of the old Abbot's House, which dates from A.D. 1376, gained its name from tapestries of the Holy City which at one time draped its walls. From Jerusalem Chamber, the preface of the Revision version of the Holy Bible was dated, and in this Chamber the far-reaching task was performed. " Where-ever " says Dr. Hensley Henson, " the Bible is studied and valued a fresh stream of interests sets towards Westminster Abbey. It is, far more than Canter-bury, the mother Church of English Christendom." John Williams, one of the greatest of Westminster's Deans, the last Churchman to hold the Great Seal and a liberal benefactor to the Abbey in Stuart times, adorned the Chamber and added much to the Library and the School. The College Hall which adjoins the old Abbot's House is of similar construction, with ancient carving. It is now used as the Dining Hall of Westminster School, the only public scholastic establishment in London occupying its ancient site.

Such is but a brief outline of Westminster Abbey—" the history of our race set in stone," a House of God reverenced the world over, loved almost equally by our kinsmen across the Atlantic, if we but take as evidence the gifts which have come to it from the United States, and also the great service held in July 1923 in honour of one of America's most honoured sons and a worthy protagonist of Anglo-American friendship—Walter Hines Page, the Ambassador to the Court of St. James in the dark days of the Great War.

ST. PAUL'S CATHEDRAL

S T. PAUL'S may rightly claim to be the Imperial Cathedral of the British nation. True, Westminster Abbey is more in the minds of men as "the State church," for within its walls kings and queens have been crowned since Harold, and since Sebert many monarchs and their consorts have there found their last resting-place. But throughout the ages it is to St. Paul's that men's minds have turned instinctively in any great time of crisis or rejoicing in the life of the Nation. It is the official church of the Empire " in a way that belongs to no other Cathedral "; it is, as it were, a spiritual centre firmly fixed in "the hub of the Universe," from which pulsates the religious life-blood, not only of the denizens of Great Britain, but of our kinsmen overseas. Like our ancestors, we have become accustomed to look to St. Paul's for the inspiration and suggestion which comes from our Faith. If an example were wanted of this, we need only recall those services during the Great War. No one then present could have failed to grasp what St. Paul's stands for to the British people. In a Cathedral sermon preached at that time, Canon Alexander rightly described it as "the Parish Church of the British Empire." As a prominent Church dignitary once said, "It has come to be considered the most fitting place for the expression of the religious emotions of the Nation."

Of the first church on this site we know little. Some authorities have it that at least four churches have crowned this mound—the highest ground in the City of London. The Rev. Lewis Gilbertson, M.A., in the authorised guide to St. Paul's Cathedral, opens with the definite statement that " the St. Paul's which we see to-day is the third cathedral which has been built, *de novo* on the site it now occupies." This fact is certain, that the history of St. Paul's is as old as that of our nation.

In the distant ages a Temple of Diana is supposed to have stood upon the site. Wren, who rejected this theory, was however of opinion, owing to certain discoveries made when excavations were in progress for his great work, that in the Roman period the Christians built a church there which was afterwards demolished by the Pagan Saxons. Stow, in his Survey of London, records that when the foundations were being prepared for a chapel on the south side of St. Paul's in 1316 " more than a hundred scalps of oxen or kine " were found ; " which thing confirms greatly the opinion of those which have reported that of old times there had been a temple of Jupiter, and that there was daily sacrifice of beasts." Roman remains, including a bronze image of Diana, have been found at intervals near St. Paul's, and, as recently as 1830, a stone altar bearing a carved figure of the goddess was unearthed on the site of the present Goldsmiths' Hall in Foster Lane.

There is, however, evidence that Christianity was rooted in London in

ST. PAUL'S CATHEDRAL

ST. PAUL'S CATHEDRAL: THE CHOIR

ST. PAUL'S CATHEDRAL: THE CHOIR STALLS AND ORGAN LOFT

ST. PAUL'S CATHEDRAL: SIR CHRISTOPHER WREN'S GRAVE IN THE CRYPT

the third century. The late Archdeacon Sinclair, whose intense love for St. Paul's was apparent to all who came in contact with him, reminds us * that about A.D. 208 Tertullian wrote " that the Kingdom and Name of Christ were then acknowledged in Britain even in those parts then accessible to the Romans." Several subsequent writers speak in terms of enthusiasm of the British church, and the Archdeacon goes on to say : " In 314 a gleam of light occurs ; a Council of Bishops was held at Arles in the south of Gaul, and was attended by three British Bishops, whose names are inscribed in the records of the Council, and of whom one was Restitutus Bishop of London.† No doubt there was a long line of these Bishops ; no doubt they had a Bishop's Church or Cathedral ; perhaps it may have been on the site of St. Paul's, but that is all that can be said."

London, no doubt, like other parts of the territory of the East Saxons, lapsed from Christianity into Paganism. "But," says the Venerable Bede,‡ " when this province (the East Saxons) also received the word of truth by the preaching of Mellitus, King Ethelbert built the Church of St. Paul in the City of London, where he (Mellitus) and his successors should have their episcopal seat." Mellitus was consecrated, according to Bede, by St. Augustine in A.D. 604. The admirable Stow gives us the following :

" Then is the north churchyard of Paules, in the which standeth the Cathedral Church first founded by Ethelbert, King of Kent, about the year of Christ 610 : he gave thereto lands as appeareth :

" ' ÆDELBERTUS REX, DEO INSPIRANTE, PRO ANIMÆ SUÆ REMEDIO DEDIT EPISCOPO MELITO TERRAM QUÆ APPELLATUR TILLINGEHAM AD MONASTERII SUI SOLATIUM, SCILICET MONASTERIUM SANCTI PAULI : ET EGO REX ÆDELBERTUS ITA FIRMITER CONCEDO TIBI PRESULI MELITO POTESTATEM EJUS HABENDI ET POSSIDENDI UT IN PERPETUUM IN MONAS- TERII UTILITATE PERMANEAT,' ETC.

" Athelstan, Edgar, Edward the Confessor, and others, also gave lands thereunto. William the Conqueror gave to the Church of St. Paule and to Mauricius, then bishop, and his successors, the castle of Stortford, with the appurtenances, etc. He also confirmed the gifts of his predecessors in these words : W. REX ANGL. CONCEDO DEO ET S. PAULO IN PERPETUUM 24 HIDAS QUAS REX ÆTHELBERT DEDIT S. PAULO JUXTA LONDON. . . ."

The land called " Tillingeham," it is interesting to note, is still held by the Dean and Chapter of St. Paul's as a sacred charge, and still fulfils the purpose for which Ethelbert the Good gave it over 1300 years ago.

Fire destroyed Ethelbert's church in A.D. 962, soon after Dunstan became Primate. In the rebuilt cathedral St. Alphege, Archbishop of Canterbury, who was beaten to death by drunken Danes, was buried in 1014, and, in the

---

* " Memorials of St. Paul's Cathedral." The Venerable William Sinclair, D.D. Chapman & Hall, London.
† The three British Bishops recorded as being present were Eborious of Eboracum, Restitutus of London, and Adelphius " de civitate colonia Londinensium."   ‡ " Eccl. Hist." Book II, c. 3.

same century, Ethelred the Unready and Edward the Outlaw were interred there also. What was probably the first great Ecclesiastical Parliament in England was held by Lanfranc, Archbishop of Canterbury, in St. Paul's in 1075, attended by Thomas, Archbishop of York, Walkelin of Winchester, Wulfstan of Worcester, and the majority of the other Bishops and the principal Abbots of the great monasteries. Archdeacon Sinclair says that the question of precedence of the Bishops was first settled, the Archbishop of York being seated on Lanfranc's right and William of London on his left—Walkelin of Winchester, as representing the oldest Saxon capital, being placed next to York.

In the fire of 1087 St. Paul's was again burnt down, while most of the City also suffered by fire. Mauritius, chaplain to the Conqueror, who had been appointed Bishop of London in succession to Hugh de Orivalle, who " died a leper," immediately commenced building a new cathedral, " A work," says Stow, " that men of that time judged would never be finished, it was so wonderful in length and breadth." Many of the contemporaries of Mauritius, such as William of Malmesbury, wrote the late Dean Milman in his " Annals of St. Paul's," " must have seen the splendid buildings erected in Normandy, at Rouen, and by the Conqueror at Caen. Yet," writes the chronicler, " such was the magnificence of its (St. Paul's) beauty, that it may be accounted among the most famous buildings. So vast was the extent of the crypt, such the capaciousness of the upper structure, that it could contain the utmost conceivable multitude of worshippers." The work began at a time when, as J. R. Green, the historian, records, " London took its full share of the great revival. The City was proud of its religion, its thirteen conventual and more than one hundred parochial churches. . . . In the midst of the City Bishop Richard (Richard de Belmeis I) busied himself with the vast cathedral which Bishop Maurice had begun ; barges came up the river with stone from Caen for the great arches that moved the popular wonder." There is in the London Museum at Stafford House, St. James's, an excellent model of St. Paul's at the time of the Great Fire of London which gives an excellent idea of the magnitude and fine exterior of that great building.

It was in this great edifice that King John publicly did homage to the Pope and handed over his kingdom, to receive it back as a vassal, and it was at St. Paul's that Langton solemnly urged the Barons to uphold the liberties of England against the Tyrant, an action which was " a prelude to Runnymede." Among the signatures on Magna Charta is that of William of Sainte Mere l'Eglise, Bishop of London. For the part that Old St. Paul's played in the life of the Nation the reader is referred to the works of Dean Milman and Archdeacon Sinclair. It must suffice here to say that it was the great bell of St Paul's which summoned the citizens to the side of Simon de Montfort against the King ; Arthur, Prince of Wales, was married in the Cathedral to Katherine of Aragon in November 1501, and in 1509 Henry VII, who had died at Richmond, was brought over London Bridge to lie in state at St. Paul's ; while Henry VIII received the Cap of Maintenance there, and Wolsey,

Cardinal Archbishop of York, sang Mass on the occasion of "the proclamation of the Eternal Peace between the Kings of France and England, the Pope, the Emperor, and the King of Spain."

Within the Cathedral precincts stood St. Paul's Cross, the great centre of open-air gatherings addressed by Latimer and other famous ecclesiastics, where the bulls of Urban IV and other Popes were promulgated, where the Pope's condemnation of Luther was proclaimed to the great gathering which included Cardinal Wolsey, and where " the Dean of Paul's accursed all those which had searched in the Church of St. Martin-in-the-Field for a hoard of gold." Eventually the famous cross, which had been for many ages the most solemn place in this nation for the greatest of divines and most eminent scholars to preach at, was levelled to the ground. This act was due to the Long Parliament in 1642, by the votes of which " the very foundation of this famous cathedral was utterly shaken in pieces." St. Paul's Cross was not as has been shown already, a place for preaching merely. Stow says that the antiquity of the folk-mote which assembled there from time to time went beyond written annals. In 1259 Henry III and his brother Richard, King of Almayne, attended one such gathering. At St. Paul's Cross Edward II received homage from the earls supporting him ; and nearly 300 years later Lord Mayor Thomas Skinner during the sermon received a message from Queen Elizabeth to raise men to assist in the defence of Calais. The great religious services grouped around this famous Cross must have been inspiring. Bishop Jewell, in the course of a letter to Peter Martyr, wrote : " You may now [1560] sometimes see at St. Paul's Cross 6000 persons old and young, of both sexes, all singing together and praising God." It is with such records in our minds that gratitude must be expressed to the late Mr. H. C. Richards, M.P., for the new St. Paul's Cross in the garden of the Cathedral.

Old St. Paul's was engaging the attention of builders owing to its decaying condition for some time before the Great Fire of London. Its great spire, practically destroyed by lightning in 1561, was never replaced. By a fund established to revive the glories of the edifice the great building was refaced inside and out under the direction of Inigo Jones. After this restoration Wren, who had become noted for his skill in building, was authorised to carry out a plan he had prepared for the thorough repair of

St. Paul's Cross

the Cathedral, and was only prevented by the Great Fire which swept the City from London Bridge to the Temple. The first intention was again to restore the Cathedral, not to rebuild. A portion of the Nave which had not been damaged to a great extent by the Fire was covered with a temporary roof ; but in 1668, through the falling of one of the piers Dean Sancroft obtained consent to build an entirely new cathedral. For the Building Fund Royal Warrants were issued authorising the Building Committee to borrow money on the security of a wine and coal tax, so that though St. Paul's received a sum exceeding £130,000 from donors in all parts of the country, says the Rev. Lewis Gilbertson, " It differs from all other cathedrals in having been built with money arising from taxation. The other cathedrals were built at the charges of private persons, by voluntary offerings made for the honour of God and to the cause of the Catholic religion ; but the destruction of Old St. Paul's, along with the many churches and other buildings which shared its fate, was regarded as a national calamity." The money realised from the tax was divided into three portions, of which St. Paul's received one, the other City churches one, and the remainder was set apart to assist private owners in rebuilding. " This fact," Mr. Gilbertson reminds us, " leads to a further differentiation of St. Paul's from other cathedral churches, in that to meet the public character of the Building Fund the fabric is vested in three trustees outside the Dean and Chapter, viz. :—The Archbishop of Canterbury, the Bishop of London, and the Lord Mayor for the time being. The Lord Mayor on this account has peculiar privileges in St. Paul's, having his own stall in the Choir and a right to look to the Cathedral for all religious offices."

Wren submitted several designs for the new Cathedral, including one in the form of a Greek cross, which the Chapter opposed. Eventually the King gave Wren " liberty, in the prosecution of his work, to make variations, rather ornamental than essential, as from time to time he should see proper, and to leave the whole to his management " ;* and, says Longman in his " Three Cathedrals," " Wren availed himself of this permission to an incredible extent, and constructed a building almost as different from the approved plan as St. Paul's Cathedral is from that of Salisbury." On May Day 1674 the clearing and levelling was commenced, a task which took two years to perform. When Wren was marking out the site for his masterpiece it is said that a labourer brought from one of the rubbish heaps a piece of stone to mark the centre of the building. The piece of stone, picked haphazard, was part of a tombstone with nothing of the inscription save the word *Resurgam*. This incident was regarded at the time as a good omen, and is stated to have prompted Cibber's sculpture over the South Transept door, representing the Phœnix rising from the flames. With complete absence of ceremony Wren laid the first stone of the present St. Paul's on June 21, 1675, his great ambition being to erect a church " which should last, not for a time but for ever." In December 1697 the Choir was opened for divine service—

* " Parentalia," p. 283.

12

the occasion being the Thanksgiving for the Peace of Ryswick—and in 1710 Wren's son, in the presence of his father and " that excellent artificer Mr. Strong, his son, and other free and accepted masons, chiefly employed in the execution of the work," laid the laſt ſtone on the top of the lantern. " It is well known," Archdeacon Sinclair points out, " that Wren was a Freemason, and that he was one of the earlier pioneers which converted the craft of practical and working freemasonry, in his day no longer needed, into its modern form of a speculative and ideal fellowship. St. Paul's was probably the laſt building erected by freemasons ; it is believed that many of his workmen belonged to the craft, and held their lodges in the neighbourhood."

All through the thirty-five years which elapsed from the laying of the firſt ſtone to the laſt, Wren worked ſteadfaſtly towards the realisation of his aim, notwithſtanding the treatment which he received from time to time from the Building Committee. " Throughout his work," writes the Rev. Lewis Gilbertson, " Wren had been pursued with a spite and bitterness which is almoſt incredible. . . . Wren's pursuers at laſt arraigned him before Parliament . . . and got an order passed withholding a moiety of his pay (which throughout the whole time of the building was only £200 a year) until the whole should be completed. Finally, in the year 1718, the eighty-sixth of his age, Wren's patent was suspended and William Benson was appointed to succeed him." Wren retired to his house at Hampton Court, returning to the Cathedral once every year to spend the day beneath the Dome in quiet contemplation of " the work which, in spite of hindrances, had been all his own." He died on February 25, 1723, and was buried near his daughter in the Crypt. For nearly a hundred and fifty years there was no other memorial to him in St. Paul's than the Latin inscription placed by his son over his grave, which, translated, reads as follows :

Nelsons' Tomb

" UNDERNEATH LIES BURIED THE BUILDER OF THIS CHURCH AND CITY, CHRISTOPHER WREN, WHO LIVED MORE THAN 90 YEARS, NOT FOR HIMSELF BUT FOR THE PUBLIC GOOD. READER, IF YOU ASK FOR A MONUMENT, LOOK ABOUT YOU."

Associated with Wren in his great creation, described as " a product of the late Renaissance, unique among English cathedrals as the only non-Gothic building of its class," were Thomas Strong of Taynton, Oxfordshire, his maſter mason ; Edward Strong, who became maſter mason on the death of Thomas ; Nicholas

Hawksmoor (famous as the builder of many London churches), who was clerk of works at 20*d*. per day ; Grinling Gibbons, to whom is due the delicate wood-carving for which St. Paul's is renowned ; and Tijou, a French artist in metal work, whose iron grilles, staircase railings and low railing in front of the Choir are masterpieces.

The cost of the great building is stated to have been approximately £1,000,000 of the money of that time. Over £800,000 was raised through the Coal Tax, and at least another £130,000 by private subscription. It is impossible to estimate what the cost would have been to-day—perhaps £5,000,000. The exterior of St. Paul's is 515 feet long, the interior 479 feet ; the total height from the pavement to the top of the Cross is 365 feet, and the width of the transepts from door to door is 250 feet. The area of the Cathedral is 84,311 square feet. In size, only four cathedrals excel St. Paul's— St. Peter's, Rome (227,000 square feet), Milan (108,277 square feet), Seville (100,000 square feet), Florence (84,802 square feet).

In viewing St. Paul's the mind is naturally attracted to the majestic dome, weighing some 60,000 tons, to all appearances one structure, but in reality composed of three shells : (1) the outward roof of wood covered with lead, (2) the intermediate brick cone which supports the lantern and its accessories of 700 tons in weight, and (3) the inside dome, also of brick. For over ten years now many workmen have been constantly engaged in the delicate and vital task of restoring the great pillars which support the Dome, and which must necessarily be in every way secure enough to ensure the safety of the building and of the public who wish to worship there. Much of the stone work has suffered badly these last two centuries—London's atmosphere is not conducive to the well-being of stone work, especially where permanency is essential.

In other parts of the Cathedral also, apart from the great piers, the eternal war against decay must be carried on. The work goes on day after day, replacing worn stones, recementing others, and so on. The piers are only 4½ feet below the level of the floor, and underneath these is sand. Wren had the most difficult of tasks to procure much of his material, and he had to be content to fill the piers with rubble, as he was always hampered for money. These foundations must be kept safe from any undermining, and part of the Cathedral has had to be closed to expedite the work.

It may interest the reader to know that nearly £130,000 has been raised for this Preservation work since 1913, and that a further appeal issued

The Wellington Monument

by the Dean and Chapter through *The Times* in January 1925 and responded to from all parts of the world has resulted in an additional sum of £250,000.

Inside the Dome, about 100 feet above the pavement, is the Whispering Gallery. An attendant whispering across the gallery can, owing to acoustic property due to the circular wall and the nearness of the concave hemisphere above, be distinctly heard. Wren had desired to have the inside face of the Dome covered with mosaics in order that the cupola might have a lighter appearance. The work was to have been undertaken by four Italian experts, but Wren was overruled, and the task of decorating the Dome with scenes in monochrome from the life of St. Paul was given to Sir James Thornhill. Some idea of what Wren's scheme would have looked like if carried out can be gathered from the magnificent mosaic work of the late Sir William Richmond, R.A., on the ceilings of both the nave and quarter domes. Sir William had for many years studied mosaic work in Italy and at St. Sophia, Constantinople. The Choir, the one-time dingy appearance of which is still within the memory of living men, has been transformed into a place of great beauty, owing to Sir William's enthusiastic revival of the art of mosaic. The cost of these mosaics is given at about £78,000. The work in the spandrels between the great arches was begun by Dr. Salviati in Dean Milman's time, from the designs of Alfred Stevens and G. F. Watts, R.A.

The Altar and Reredos, the latter the subject of controversy and litigation in the closing decades of last century, is in white Parian marble, with bands and panels of Rosso Antico, Verde di Prato, and Brescia marble, and is reverently crowned by a figure of the risen Christ. The prevailing idea of the sculptured subjects is the Incarnation and Life of Our Lord. The Cross below is adorned with precious stones and lapis lazuli. The massive copper candlesticks are copies of those at Ghent, which are said to have been taken from Old St. Paul's and sold by Parliamentarians at the time of the Protectorate. The beautifully carved choir stalls are the work of Grinling Gibbons, which originally cost over £1300, and, both in conception and detail, the carving is a lasting credit to the woodworkers of their day.

The Lectern takes the familiar form of an eagle, and is of bronze. This fine piece of work was finished in 1720 by one Jacob Sutton at a cost of £241 14s.

The Pulpit, a memorial to Captain Robert FitzGerald, was designed by Penrose. It is

Chapel of St. Michael and St. George

15

made of marble, of which the grey is from Plymouth, the dark purplish from Anglesey, and the red from Cork. The green is from Tenos, the yellow from Siena, with a little of the ancient Giallo Antico from Rome.

In the opening stages of this chapter mention was made of the connection between St. Paul's and the Empire, a connection which is emphasised to a considerable degree by the beautiful Chapel of the Order of St. Michael and St. George—the Order of the Colonies and the Empire—which stands in the south-west corner of the Cathedral. The Order, of which the Prince of Wales is the present head, became an Order for the British Colonies in general " for such natural-born subjects of the Crown of the United Kingdom as may have held or shall hold high and confidential offices within Her Majesty's colonial possessions, or in reward for services to the Crown in relation to the foreign affairs of the Empire." The Chapel, at one time the London Consistory Court, where a number of celebrated cases were heard, including the famous application to open the Druce vault is beautifully panelled and draped with the banners of the members of the Order. Here on St. George's Day the members of the Order assemble in memory of those members who have died during the year. The Chapel is, in the words of Archdeacon Sinclair, to whom was due the initial step which led to accommodation being found for the Order at St. Paul's, " the shrine of the Knightly Brotherhood who have devoted their lives to the service of the Empire in Colonial Lands."

The Crypt includes one of the oldest British churches—St. Faith's, incorporated in the Cathedral in 1255. Many famous men are buried here. Nelson rests beneath the centre of the Dome in a sarcophagus originally intended for Cardinal Wolsey, and afterwards taken by Henry VIII to Windsor, from whence it was brought to St. Paul's for the remains of our greatest naval hero, which were enclosed in a coffin made from a portion of a mast of " L'Orient." Also buried here, in a tomb of Cornish porphyry, is the Iron Duke, whose great funeral car, made of guns melted down at Woolwich, stands at the west end of the Crypt. There are also the tombs of Lord Napier of Magdala, Lord Roberts, Lord Wolseley, Sir Henry Wilson, whose valuable life was cut short by assassins in 1922 ; Lord Leighton, Sir Joshua Reynolds, and Sir Thomas Lawrence, all three Presidents of the Royal Academy ; Benjamin West, Sir John Millais, Sir J. Edgar Boehm, J. M. W. Turner, Holman Hunt, George Cruikshank, W. E. Henley, the essayist, Sir Walter Besant, Charles Reade, Admiral Lord Collingwood, and three well-known figures at St. Paul's, Bishop Creighton, Dean Milman and Canon Liddon. Thomas Attwood, Maurice Greene, and William Boyce, celebrated organists of St. Paul's, lie side by side with Sir Arthur Sullivan. Close to the entrance is a medallion portrait of Captain Scott, the Antarctic explorer, who perished in a blizzard returning from the South Pole in 1912.

Memorials are to be seen, both here and in the Nave, to famous scientists, engineers, men renowned in the medical profession, famous ecclesiastics, poets, and dramatists ; to Lord Mayo, Governor-General of India, murdered during his term of office, to General Gordon, killed at Khartoum, and to Sir Bartle

Frere, known for his work during troublous times in South Africa. Conspicuous among them is Stevens' great monument to the Duke of Wellington, the bronze portions of which were made from French cannon taken in his campaigns. Almost opposite is the memorial to Lord Roberts. A beautiful memorial tablet to Florence Nightingale ensures that the noble profession of Nursing is not forgotten.

A recent addition in the Crypt of particular interest to our American cousins is a memorial bust of Washington, presented by the American nation and unveiled by Mr. George Brinton Harvey, American Ambassador 1921–23. There is also a bust of Sir John Alexander MacDonald, the first Premier of Canada. Not very far away, a beautiful memorial recalls the sacrifices of the Dominion troops in the South African campaign, and Captain Cook, the great explorer, is remembered in another fine group. Famous war correspondents, including Russell of *The Times*, are commemorated here. These are but a few of the memorials contained in St. Paul's.

A tablet tells of famous people interred in the Crypt of Old St. Paul's—such as Sebba, King of the East Saxons, who was buried here in A.D. 677 ; Ethelred, King of the Angles, 1017 ; John of Gaunt, Duke of Lancaster, 1399 ; Sir Anthony Van Dyck, the celebrated painter, 1641 ; also no less than twenty-eight Bishops of London found a last resting-place in this sacred area, from Erkenwald, son of Offa, King of Saxons, the third Bishop of London, who died about 685. In the Nave are to be seen three well-known pictures. Two are by G. F. Watts, " Peace and Goodwill " and " Time, Death and Judgment." The other is W. Holman Hunt's famous work " The Light of the World," a replica of the picture at Keble College, Oxford. Romanelli's ' Dead Christ " is in the south choir aisle.

The Library over the south-west chapel contains Luther's own Bible and a small volume giving the list of subscriptions promised for the building of Wren's cathedral. The list is headed by the signature of Charles II promising £1000 a year. " Alas ! " says Dr. Sinclair, " it was not paid." On another page James, Duke of York, after James II, promised " £200 a year, to begin from Midsummer last passed." This was paid. A portion of Wren's building account is also to be seen. There is another volume containing the signatures of Laud, William Juxon, who as Bishop of London attended Charles I on the scaffold, and Lord Clarendon. Cranmer's signature is also preserved in a book ; and there is the writ appointing Doctor Tait as Bishop of London in 1856, bearing the autograph of Queen Victoria.

St. Paul's possesses what is considered to be the finest peal of bells in the world. The peal, which is in the north tower, consists of twelve bells, the cost of which was defrayed by the City of London, the late Baroness Burdett-Coutts, and the Worshipful Companies of Drapers, Turners, Salters, Merchant Tailors, Grocers, Cloth Workers, and Fishmongers. In the south-west tower is the old State bell, originally cast at the time of Edward I, known first as " Edward of Westminster " and afterwards as " Westminster Tom," presented to St. Paul's by William III. This bell, still tolled on the death

of any member of the Royal family, weighs 11,474 pounds. "Great Paul,"
placed in the tower in 1882, weighs 37,483 pounds. The Latin inscription on
Great Paul was by Canon Liddon, " Woe is me if I preach not the Gospel."
(Dr. Sinclair says the translation given by Liddon was, " May I be cracked
if I don't call the people to Church.")

It would not be fitting in closing any review of St. Paul's to omit a reference
to the music for which the Cathedral is famous. In the opinion of Gounod
the choral celebration at St. Paul's is the finest eucharistic service in the world.
The long list of organists and choir-masters contains the names of men outstanding as masters of British organ and choir music—Morley, Maurice Greene,
Thomas Attwood, Sir John Goss, Sir John Stainer, Sir G. C. Martin among
them. The organ, which was rebuilt by Mr. H. Willis from the specification
of the late Sir G. C. Martin, has 4822 speaking pipes and 76 sounding stops,
with 26 couplers and 5 rows of keys, besides the pedal board.

Detail of Carving under a window at St. Paul's

SOUTHWARK CATHEDRAL: THE NAVE

SOUTHWARK CATHEDRAL: THE SCREEN

Facing page 19

SOUTHWARK CATHEDRAL

THERE seems much approaching the symbolical in the situation of St. Saviour's Cathedral, Southwark. The Churches of all creeds and nationalities aim to bring " the Peace that passeth all understanding." St. Saviour's stands, as it were, in a secluded bay, past which swirls and eddies the sea of the multi-sided twentieth-century commercial life. It is a haven of rest, within those portals the mind is lifted above things mundane, oblivious to the roar and bustle of traffic which crosses that world-famous avenue to the heart of the great Metropolis— London Bridge. St. Saviour's seems to cry out above the maelstrom : " Is it nothing to You, all Ye that pass by ? "

Throughout the ages millions have passed by this historic church. From very remote times it stood, as Westminster Abbey stood higher up the river, close by a ferry, across which people entered and left London. As will be shown later, St. Saviour's owes its foundation to such a situation. But in thinking of St. Saviour's the mind instinctively turns to those days when at

> " *Southwerk, at this gentil hostelrye*
> *That highte the Tabard, faste by the Belle,*"

" Britain's first poet, famous Chaucer," assembled his picturesque pilgrims for their journey to Canterbury. Or, again, to even earlier times, when London Bridge was " broken down " by Olaf to stem the onslaught of the Danes, of which St. Olave's Wharf is a reminder to this day.

Then, too, within a short distance of St. Saviour's, William Shakespeare took up his residence when the Globe Theatre was opened in 1599—a spot hallowed in Literature by his works, which have made England famous and immortalised his name. The poet had made a short stay in the district previously when performing in Henslowe's " Rose." Here at Southwark were associated with Shakespeare, John Fletcher and Philip Massinger ; the former, when Shakespeare laid down his pen, being regarded as the leading dramatist of the time. One does not forget also Ben Johnson, Richard Burbage, and Alleyn of the theatrical fraternity.

These and other associations were recalled in the address presented to King Edward VII and Queen Alexandra on the occasion of the re-opening of the Cathedral in 1905, during the progress of restoration :

" . . . We need not remind your Majesties that we are standing on classic ground—the place where Shakespeare made England famous, whose younger brother was buried here in company with Massinger and Fletcher —a place of literary renown long before then, in the days of Gower, who rests among us, and Chaucer, whose Canterbury Pilgrims set out from the Tabard Inn, once close at hand."

19

Southwark Cathedral—although it has not yet reached its majority as the Mother Church of a See—has a history extending over more than a thousand years of the eventful life of the British nation. Roman tiles to be seen in the Nave are a testimony to the antiquity of the site, for here probably stood during the Occupation one of the Roman temples.

It is, however, from the period before the commencement of Westminster Abbey, and soon after the foundation of the diocese of Winchester, that we first have some idea of the early ecclesiastical history of the district. We read that before the first London Bridge was built (that is presuming that the Romans never had a bridge connection here) "a certain Mary founded a house of Sisters to maintain a ferry over the Thames." The ferry gave to the Nunnery the name of "St. Mary Overie," a title which the present Cathedral Church bore until the Dissolution. (Overie, the concise guide to the Cathedral issued by the S.P.C.K. suggests, may mean "of the ferry," "over the river," or, perhaps, "of the bank.")

The Rev. T. P. Stevens, until recently succentor and sacrist of St. Saviour's, suggests in his entertaining and instructive work "The Story of Southwark Cathedral," that students should regard the early history of the foundation as rather vague and legendary. "We are" he says, "on safer ground when we reach the ninth century, when St. Swithun, Bishop of Winchester, dissolved the convent and established in its place a College of Priests." St. Swithun had jurisdiction in Southwark because at that time and, in fact, until 1877 parts of South London came within the borders of the diocese of Winchester."

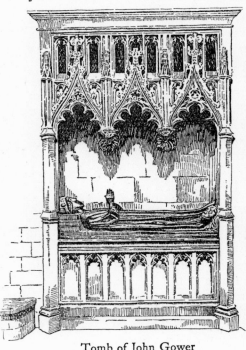

Tomb of John Gower

In 1106 the "secular" collegiate clergy were supplanted by Canons Regular of St. Augustine, or "Black Canons," a body of "religious" which was founded at Avignon in 1061. The Mother House in England was established at Colchester in 1106, just before the change at Southwark. The change is attributed by some to William Gifford, founder of Waverley Abbey (the *Waverley* of Sir Walter Scott) and Bishop of Winchester, while other authorities incline to the view that the secular clergy themselves adopted the rule of the Augustinian Order. Aldgod was the first Prior, the Founders being two Norman knights, William Pont de la Arch and William Dauncy. With the change came the building of a Norman church under the guidance of Gifford, parts of which are still visible to-day in the entrance to the Chapel of St. John the Divine—the

20

Harvard Chapel—while a Norman recess and a doorway can be seen in the north aisle towards the west.

To the west of the Priory, Gifford also erected Winchester House, where in after years Henry VIII met Catharine Howard. Winchester House must have been a stately palace in its heyday. Stow describes it as " a very fair house, well repaired and hath a large wharf and landing place, called the Bishop of Winchester stair." It was separated from the Priory and St. Mary Overy's Church by St. Saviour's Dock in the sixteenth century, and judging from the excellent drawings of London Bridge and its surroundings recently published by *The Builder*, the Bishop's Palace and conventual buildings must have been striking in character.

During the episcopacy of Peter de la Roche a Choir and Retro-Choir and a Chapel, dedicated to St. Mary Magdalene Overie for the use of parishioners, were begun, and a Hospital, afterwards dedicated to Saint Thomas Becket, was built on a site on which it remained until 1862, when, to make room for the railway, it was transferred to Walworth, and from thence to its present fine situation facing the Thames, opposite the Houses of Parliament.

There is in the Cathedral a famous monument (1408) to John Gower, a friend of Chaucer, poet, lawyer, courtier, and a great benefactor to the Priory which earned him the following :

> " *This Church was rebuilt by John Gower, the rhymer,*
> *Who in Richard's gay court was a fortunate climber,*
> *Should anyone start, 'tis right he should know it,*
> *Our wight was a lawyer as well as a poet.*"

Gower built a beautiful chantry, which, like many others in this country, was destroyed at the time of the Dissolution. Cardinal Beaufort, at this time restored the south transept. The principal addition in the sixteenth century was a fine altar screen by Bishop Fox, who was Bishop of Winchester during the office of the last Prior, Bartholomew Linstede, and took a keen interest in the second Church in his See. It recalls the well-known altar screen or reredos at Winchester Cathedral. Originally it was exceedingly ornate, but suffered much by the erection of a wooden screen over it in 1703, when the mediæval stonework with its ancient niches was ruthlessly dealt with. For many years this gem of church ornamentation was lost to sight behind woodwork and mortar, until between 1830 and 1839 the wooden screen was removed and the glories of the stonework were once more apparent. Its restoration was carried out by Mr. Robert Wallace, but when the reredos left his hand it was still a frame without a picture, for no figures had ever adorned it. During the last twenty years small figures of the twelve Apostles have been inserted, and many larger figures have been set up, which tell in stone the story of Southwark and its religious leaders—so thoughtfully have they been chosen. The screen will bear deliberate inspection and study, so well does it epitomise the history of the Borough ; and at the same time it contains some work of outstanding beauty. The visitor will recognise the figure of King Edward VII. who laid the foundation-stone of the new nave in 1890, attended the re-opening of the church in 1897, and was present in 1905 at the inauguration of the church as a cathedral. There are also statues of Bishop Talbot, the first Bishop of Southwark, Bishop Thorold, who as Bishop of Rochester initiated, in 1889, the re-building of the nave, the present Archbishop of Canterbury, who succeeded Dr. Thorold as Bishop of Rochester, Cardinal Beaufort, William of Wykeham, Bishop Gifford, and St. Swithun of Winchester, all of whom were ultimately associated with Southwark's Church.

The Choir, the Rev. T. P. Stevens points out, is part of the thirteenth-century church, and it is fortunate that a proposal made in 1831, that the whole church should be demolished and a new one added to the tower, was successfully opposed, and that the task of restoration was superintended by Mr. George Gwilt, the famous architect. Mr. Gwilt kept well in view the older work, so that the east end resembles its pristine appearance. In the wall at the east end of the triforium are two roundheaded doorways, now unseen but still *in situ*, which may reasonably be taken to indicate that parts of the old Norman structure were retained in the walls of the Choir as it now stands.

As already stated, the Nave was rebuilt as the outcome of the endeavours of Bishop Thorold. The old nave was built in Gothic style in 1206. The roof was of stone, and collapsed in 1469. A decorated wooden roof which replaced it was found to be in a dangerous condition in 1830. No funds being available for repair, it was taken down, thus leaving the body of the church unprotected for nine years, when a temporary structure was erected in its place, which was used until the necessary funds were forthcoming for the restoration commenced in 1889. Sir Arthur Blomfield in his designs generally followed out the earlier nave, with its round and octagonal pillars alternating on the old foundations. A considerable amount of the old masonry is to be seen in the west wall. The windows of the Nave, of great interest, include those to Chaucer, Shakespeare, Fletcher, Massinger, Beaumont, Alleyn, Goldsmith, Johnson, Sacheverell, Bunyan, and Cruden (the compiler of the Concordance). The Great West Window, the work of Mr. Henry Holiday, presents the story of the Creation.

The Lady Chapel, or Retro-Choir, underwent a number of vicissitudes from the time of Queen Elizabeth until the reign of Charles I. In the latter half of the sixteenth century the parish became so poor that the treasures of the church were sold, while the chapel, in order to find funds for the parish school, was rented to a baker until 1625, when it was cleaned and restored to its proper usages. Further restoration was necessary in 1832, and the parishioners decided by vote to demolish the chapel. Leading architects roused public feeling in favour of the fabric, and succeeded in saving a chapel which is to-day a worthy reminder of the peak-point of Gothic architecture.

The Lady Chapel has four aisles, from the third of which, until 1830, a chapel projected, called " The Little Lady Chapel," or " The Bishop's Chapel," containing as it did the tomb of Bishop Lancelot Andrewes. Beneath the windows at the end of the first aisle is a strange figure, the head of which points

SOUTHWARK CATHEDRAL: THE LADY CHAPEL

SOUTHWARK CATHEDRAL: HARVARD CHAPEL

to the representation being that of a monk, which the Rev. T. P. Stevens considers was probably a *memento mori*. On the south side of the chapel are windows containing scenes from the experiences of the Marian martyrs—Bishop Hooper, of Gloucester and Worcester, Bishop Robert Ferrar, of St. David's, Prebendaries John Rogers, John Bradford and Rowland Taylor, and the Rev. Laurence Saunders—condemned to death in the chapel in 1555 ; while the three-light window in the north wall venerates Charles I, Thomas Becket, and William Laud. (There is also another window to Becket over the Canons' vestry door.) To be seen in the chapel also are fine examples of the Decorated school and the Perpendicular style. Behind the new War Memorial—a fine St. George and the Dragon by Mr. J. N. Comper—is a beautiful octagonal pillar only recently covered up. It is one of the original pillars of the choir going back to the days when, at the west end, there was no altar screen, but, instead, two open arches, which led into the chapel we are describing. Of pathetic interest is the plain lectern with its two books, bearing the initials " A. A." 1885, a testimony to the heroism of a little servant girl, Alice Ayres, who, after saving the lives of three of her employer's children in a fire, fell exhausted into the street and died of her injuries—one of those noble deeds which glorify womanhood, and an epic of " mean streets."

St. Saviour's has a particular attraction for our American cousins, for within its walls in 1607 was baptised John Harvard, the founder of the great University of the United States. To his honour the Harvard Chapel was erected in Gothic style, according to the plans of Mr. C. R. Blomfield, the entire cost being defrayed by the members of the University. Mr. Joseph Choate, the revered ambassadorial representative of Washington at the Court of St. James, gave a memorial window in 1905. The chapel was built upon the site of an old Norman chapel, of which interesting portions are retained. On the north wall is a coat of arms with the initials " A. R.," and near the western pillar is a sword-rest, recalling the visits of Queen Anne to the church to hear the famous Southwark preacher, Dr. Sacheverell. There is also among the monuments in the Cathedral one to William Emerson (1575), an ancestor of Ralph Waldo Emerson.

The Cathedral contains a number of interesting monuments in addition to those already described. There is one to Shakespeare, " an inhabitant of this parish," unveiled in 1912 by Sir Sidney Lee; in the Choir is a stone to Edmund Shakespeare, " a player " and brother of William, and the memories of Fletcher and Massinger, the seventeenth-century dramatists, are also perpetuated. In the Sanctuary is the tomb of the great Winchester bishop, Prelate of the Order of the Garter, Lancelot Andrewes. Bishop Sandall of Winchester was also buried in the Cathedral ; Edward Dyer, friend of Sir Philip Sidney and author of the poem " My Mind to Me a Kingdom is," is among the many others who find fitting commemoration here.

WINCHESTER CATHEDRAL

THE Cathedral Church of the Holy Trinity is so enwrapped in the history of Winchester—at one time supreme in England—as to call for some brief reference to the infancy of the city itself. The white chalk hills which embosom Winchester suggest the name " Caer Gwent " (the White City), given to the town by the Celts. It may perhaps have meant " a market town." It was certainly a town before the Romans came. To the Romans, who occupied it about the middle of the first century A.D., it became known as Venta Belgarum, and to the Saxons as Wintonceaster. There are many absurd legends as to the early history of the city. Even the British King Arthur is said to have been connected with it ; and the mediæval " Round Table," now in the castle, was supposed to date from his time. It was repaired for Henry VIII. Of the Roman period traces were discovered in the course of excavations for the castle which was intended for Charles II, when coins of Constantine the Great were unearthed ; since then portions of mosaic pavements and more coins have been found.

Camden, in his " Britannia," tells how, in the Saxon Heptarchy, the West Saxon kings lived in the city " and adorned it with magnificent churches and an episcopal see." There is no doubt that the city exercised a great and beneficent influence on the growth of Christianity in the south of England. T. E. Warton in his fascinating book (1760), " A Description of the City and College and Cathedral of Winchester," says that under King Athelstan Winchester had six mints for the coinage of money. Edgar set forth that the standard weights and measures should be " such as is observed at London and at Winchester." Egbert, when crowned King of all Britain, made Winchester his capital. Alfred the Great brought the city fame by making it a centre of learning which attracted such scholars as St. Grimbald and Asser, of St. David's. It was here that the Anglo-Saxon Chronicle was written. Cnut made it his seat of government, while Edward the Confessor was crowned in the minster founded by Alfred, just to the north of the site of the Cathedral.

The short distance between Winchester and Southampton led William the Conqueror to make the city his capital also, and, as in Saxon times, the royal treasure was kept there, for we read that at the Conqueror's death Rufus hastened to seize it. The city became exceedingly prosperous in the twelfth century as one of the first centres of the woollen trade, and many traders were attracted hither by the establishment of St. Giles's Fair by William II in a charter to Walkelin. In the time of King Stephen and the Empress Matilda Winchester suffered much by fire. Richard Cœur de Lion was crowned a second time at the Cathedral after his ransom. Henry III, who was born at Winchester, often spent Christmas there. As a seat of government Winchester began to wane during his reign, and the prosperity of the city to

24

SALISBURY

BATH AND WELLS

BRISTOL

WINCHESTER

decline also. Henry VII's eldest son, Arthur, was born in the Castle and christened in the Cathedral. Mary I and Philip of Spain were married in the Cathedral in 1554. The city was visited by James I and Charles II. Winchester fell, after a short siege, into the hands of Cromwell in 1645, whose forces did much damage to the Cathedral and destroyed the Castle. Charles II stayed frequently at the Deanery, and began to build a palace on the western hill.

The first church, on the site of which the venerable Cathedral now stands, was fancied to have been a monastic building founded by the mythical Lucius, King of the Britons, in A.D. 164. This church, some writers report, " was destroyed in the persecution of Diocletian, A.D. 206 "; that " it was afterwards restored and underwent various revolutions ; till Kygelise (? Cynegils), the first Christian King of the West Saxons, began the Cathedral in A.D. 611, which was probably finished by his successor Kenewalch and replenished with religious by Birinus, the Bishop and Apostle of the West Saxons, A.D. 646." " Soon afterwards, viz. A.D. 660," says Warton, " the see of Dorchester [sic Wessex], now in Oxfordshire, was removed thither, and Winé was appointed the first Bishop. But before this new condition was commenced Birinus and Agilbertus were the two first bishops of Winchester."

J. R. Green, in his " Short History of the English People," writes : " The old bishop stool of the West Saxons had been established by Birinus at what was then the Royal City of Dorchester (on the Thame). It remained the capital of the see of Wessex from A.D. 634 to A.D. 737, when the see was transferred to Winchester, to which place the body of St. Birinus, the apostle of Wessex, was removed." The first Bishop of Winchester was Birinus ; the second and third were Agilbert (650) and Winé (662).

Warton, who cites as one of his sources of information a manuscript of Anthony à Wood, preserved in the Ashmolean Museum at Oxford, states that the chapter of the foundation at Winchester, who were seculars, continued about 300 years, and " were at length removed by the Persuasion of Bishop Æthelwold, in the reign of King Edgar, about A.D. 963, who substituted a convent of the Benedictines, which remained until the Reformation." This was embraced in the great reforms of the famous Dunstan.

St. Swithun, around whose feast day has grown the legend concerning the weather for forty days after July 15, enlarged the first cathedral, and Æthelwold and Ælphege built a second Cathedral, which was replaced by a new Cathedral by Bishop Walkelin,

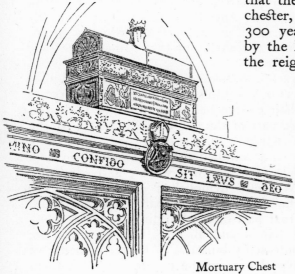

Mortuary Chest

25

the first Norman Prelate of Winchester, which comprises a large portion of the glorious edifice as we see it to-day.

"The annals of the Church of Winchester from the year A.D. 633 to A.D. 1277 compiled by a monk of Winchester," derived largely from the Cottonian MS., contains the following :

"It is said (A.D. 1086) that the King granted to Bishop Walkelin for the completion of the church of Winchester as much timber of the forest of Harpeninges as he could get, with the aid of carpenters, in four days and nights. The whole wood was felled within the given time and carried to Winchester. After this the King came to Harpeninges and looking about him, as if bewildered, he exclaimed ' Am I bewitched ? or am I beside myself ? Where am I ? Had I not a delightful wood near Winchester ?' As soon as he had found out what had been done, he became exasperated. Thereupon Walkelin snatched an old cope, demanded to see the King and fell at his feet imploring him to take back the Bishopric. ' Reserve for me with your friendship,' he cried, ' the office which I have long held in your chapel.' The King replied ' I have been too lavish a donor ; and thou hast been too greedy an acceptor.' So then he made his peace with the King, and friendship being renewed, he returned to his bishopric."

Arches in
North Transept

Walkelin's grasp of his task as builder has given us at Winchester the longest cathedral church in England—its length, close upon 556 feet, exceeding that of St. Alban's Abbey. The Cathedral had so far advanced that, in A.D. 1093, "the monks in the presence of almost all the Bishops and Abbots of England passed with much state and triumph from the old Monastery to the new one on the feast of their patron St. Swithun, and, in a most solemn procession, translated the shrine of that Saint to the new church."

Warton considers himself persuaded that " the two low built Iles at the East End of the Choir existed before the time of Walkelin, and are part of the old Church erected by the Saxon Kings . . . for they are in a more simple and confined style of architecture than any part of Walkelin's work ; and admitting that Walkelin demolished great part of the old Church, it seems probable that he should leave that part of the building in which many Saxon Kings and Bishops, his predecessors, are confessedly buried. Another evidence of this hypothesis are the crypts on which these

26

WINCHESTER CATHEDRAL: WAYNFLETE'S CHANTRY

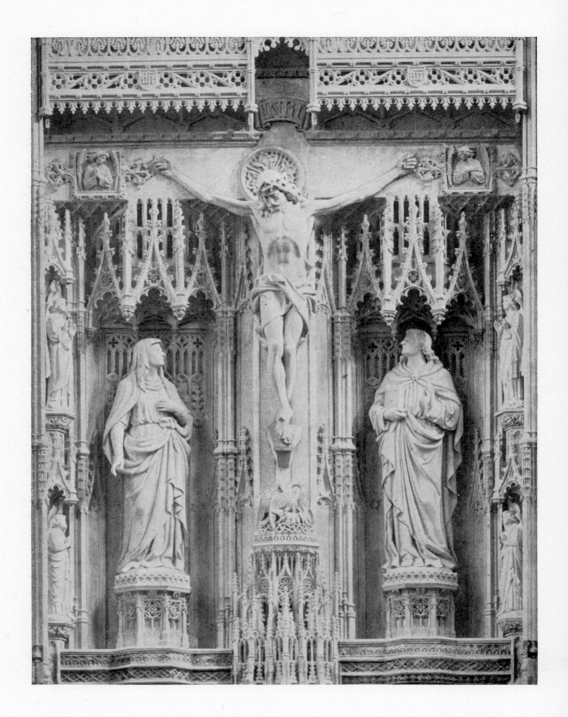

WINCHESTER CATHEDRAL: A SECTION OF THE REREDOS

low Iles stand this day, and which as appears from a Latin Epistle in verse of Wolfstan, Precentor of the Church, to Ælphege, Bishop of Winchester, A.D. 946, were constructed by Æthelwold in the Reign of King Edgar."

It is to the famous William of Wykeham that we owe much of the Cathedral as it exists to-day, and whose work embodied a part of that of his predecessor Walkelin. Walkelin's tower fell in A.D. 1107, said in those days to be the outcome of the Divine wrath because of the burial of William Rufus within the sacred precincts. The fine original Norman work is to be seen in both transepts. Prior to Wykeham, Bishop Edendon (A.D. 1346–1366) commenced the transformation of the nave and the aisles, a task completed by Wykeham. Lowth, in his life of Wykeham, speaking of the middle aisle, writes : " This aisle was originally of Saxon architecture, not greatly differing from the Roman ; with round pillars much stronger than Doric or Tuscan, or square piers adorned with small pillars ; round-headed arches and windows ; and plain walls on the outside without buttresses ; as appears by the cross-aisle and tower which remains to this day." Wykeham found the Nave " so decayed and infirm or else so mean in its appearance and so much below the dignity of one of the first episcopal sees in the Kingdom, that he determined to take down the whole of the Tower westward and to rebuild it both in stronger and more magnificent manner."

Wykeham's work began in A.D. 1394, with William Wynford as architect, Simon Membury as surveyor of the work on Wykehams' behalf, and John Wayte, a monk, representing the Convent. The massive columns of the Nave are evidence that Wykeham preserved the Norman work by casing the columns. In removing the triforium arches he transformed the Nave into a great example of Perpendicular work. Wykeham's plan for the rest of the Church was adhered to by Bishops Beaufort, Waynflete, and Fox.

At the western end of the North aisle of the Nave is to be seen the eleventh-century piece of iron grille work, the oldest example of its kind in England. A fine specimen of Norman work is the old font (A.D. 1180), its square sides being sculptured with scenes from the life of St. Nicholas of Myra. In the South aisle are the exquisite chantries of Edendon and Wykeham. On the eastern side of the South transept, which with the North transept form the oldest parts of the Cathedral, is " good Prior Silkstede's " Chapel (fifteenth century). " The spot is not consecrated by the remains of the Prior himself," says the writer of " Picturesque Memorials of Winchester," which are supposed by Milner to be interred at the back of the altar before " the Holy Hole " ;

The Font

but on a large flat stone nearly opposite the entrance is an inscription which, in the sight of many, would confer as much honour on any place of sepulture as the trophies of a mitred abbot : " HERE RESTETH THE BODY OF MR. IZAAK WALTON, WHO DIED ON THE 15TH OF DECEMBER, 1683." In the South transept is the old monastic settle and the Bishop Wilberforce monument.

The Choir, in the Decorated style, is largely due to Bishop Edendon, whose building was stopped by the Black Death until the time of Bishop Fox (A.D. 1525), the prelate who caused the remains of the Anglo-Saxon kings, Cynegils, Cynewalh, Egbert, Æthelwulf, Cnut and Queen Emma (Cnut's consort) to be collected and placed in six mortuary chests, now in the Presbytery. Fox erected the screens on either side of the Choir, and was responsible for the reconstruction of the apse in Perpendicular style. At the time of the Civil War the altar screen, Warton tells us, " was artfully protected from the violence of the Presbyterians by means of an extemporaneous wall of the partition erected in parallel line just before it, so as entirely to conceal its beauties from the observation of sacrilegious intruders."

The reredos behind the High Altar, of fifteenth- and sixteenth-century workmanship, extends over the full width of the Choir and shows Perpendicular Gothic at its best. The Choir stalls and misereres are particularly quaint. The much-discussed tomb of William Rufus is to be seen in the centre of the Choir. Behind the reredos, between the chantry of Cardinal Beaufort, the powerful son of John of Gaunt, and that of William of Waynflete, the founder of Magdalen College, Oxford, was the stone base which once supported the shrine of St. Swithun studded with jewels, the gift of King Edgar, which was destroyed in A.D. 1538. The Lady Chapel, which forms the extreme eastern end of the Cathedral, is principally the work of Bishop Godfrey de Lucy (A.D. 1189–1204), with alterations by Priors Hunton and Silkstede in the fifteenth and sixteenth centuries. The visitor will linger over the exquisite chantries in the Nave, some of which contain unrivalled specimens of sculpture, of which Winchester is rightly proud. In Gardiner's chapel is to be seen the chair on which Queen Mary sat during the solemnisation of her marriage with Philip of Spain. This was but one of the many royal ceremonies of which Winchester Cathedral has been the scene from the time when Ynewulf, the King of Wessex, was buried on the site in A.D. 755.

Considerable anxiety was occasioned in 1905 by manifestations of the insecurity of the foundations of the Cathedral. Extensive restoration was undertaken under the direction of Sir T. G. Jackson, Bart., R.A., much of which involved work by divers, under Sir Francis Fox, in consequence of the old foundations having been laid on tree-trunks in water-logged soil. The foundations were underpinned with concrete, and the Cathedral rendered secure as the outcome of over five years of patient labour.

Winchester itself will repay a thorough investigation by the visitor. King Alfred was buried at Hyde Abbey, a site now partly covered by the tower of St. Bartholomew's Church. There is also to be seen the reconstructed castle of Norman or perhaps earlier date, for many years a royal palace, wherein sat the first Parliament of 1265, and the State trial of Sir Walter Raleigh took place. There is also King Arthur's Round Table, which legend pretends was actually used by Arthur and his knights. In Winchester Alfred the Great directed the writing of the English Chronicle. At the ancient Hospital of St. Cross, which was founded by Henry of Blois in A.D. 1136 to provide board and lodging for 13 poor men and a dinner daily for 100 others, the wayfarer's dole, consisting of a horn of beer and a piece of bread, is given to all comers upon knocking at the porter's lodge. There is also Wykeham's famous College, the most ancient and one of the greatest public schools in England, with a fine chapel and cloisters.

Statue of King Alfred the Great at Winchester

SALISBURY CATHEDRAL

ALISBURY CATHEDRAL is not only endowed with surpassing beauty, but there is no trace of foreign influence perceptible in its design. It remains what it was on the day the spire was finally completed—the most perfect realisation of pure English Gothic. If the existing building had been, like its predecessor, "set on a hill," it would have formed one of the most imposing landmarks in the Kingdom. As it is, the top of the octagonal spire (404 feet from the ground) is considerably higher than the ramparts of Old Sarum Hill. Salisbury Cathedral rises majestically from a level expanse of green sward encircled by rows of giant elms and limes, and surrounded by walls (broken, here and there, by ancient gateways) constructed to a large extent from stone which once did duty at Old Sarum. It is difficult to say whether the Close derives more beauty from the Cathedral, or the Cathedral from the Close. The harmony between them is complete, and few jarring notes are to be found in the " homes of ancient peace " which have for long years existed in the shadow of the loftiest pinnacle in all England —one of the foremost glories of " Wonderful Wessex." Dr. St. Clair Donaldson, the present tenant of the Palace, in which James II tarried in fear and trembling while his son-in-law and successor was at Exeter, bears an honoured name. It is manifestly in the fitness of things that the sixty-fifth holder of the See in succession to Richard Poore should be a man of learning and of wisdom. Portions of several of the houses in the Close are of mediæval origin. The " King's house," a gabled fourteenth-century dwelling, now does duty as a training-school for women teachers, and behind the tall trees, which form a natural screen, a glimpse is caught of other time-mellowed mansions like the " King's Wardrobe " and the town-house of the Mompessons, one of whom was the original from which Philip Massinger (a native of Wilton) drew his picture of Sir Giles Overreach. In the dark days of the autumn of 1651 Charles II paid a flying visit to Salisbury Close, when Humphrey Henchman (then one of the Canons, and afterwards Bishop of Salisbury and London) rendered him valuable assistance on his perilous journey from Trent to Shoreham. The quaint gabled house on the north side of the Close has been the home of some number of *literati*, amongst whom were Archdeacon Coxe, the historian, and William Lisle Bowles, the first of the " Nature poets," whose poetry is said to have had a great influence over the productions of Wordsworth, Coleridge, and Southey. A part of the house is coeval with the Cathedral, and dates back to the thirteenth century. Henry Fielding lived for a while in a still existing house near St. Anne's Gate. Here he wrote a portion of " Tom Jones," taking Hele, the master of the Close Grammar School, where Joseph Addison, when a " rickety child," received his early education, as a model for his immortal Thwackum.

SALISBURY CATHEDRAL

SALISBURY CATHEDRAL: THE CHOIR AND WEST NAVE

Such are a very few of the memories which crowd in upon the pilgrim, as he stands by St. Anne's Gate and thinks of the kings, statesmen, bishops, and divines of a lesser degree who have passed through it both before and after the days of Fielding and Addison. If the visitor happens to be an enthusiastic Trollopian, he may, like Mr. A. G. Bradley, one of the ablest describers of this portion of Wessex, prefer frankly to cast the reminiscences of Plantagenet, Tudor, Stuart, and even Georgian sovereigns and bishops aside, and conjure up visions of early Victorian days, when the novelist installed one Dr. Proudie on the episcopal throne of Barchester, sketching in the accessories from a profound knowledge of Salisbury in general and the Close in particular. " I see," writes the author of " Round about Wiltshire," " old Mr. Harding, the venerable silver-haired ex-warden, tottering across the Close to his last service in the Cathedral, or the tall dignified figure and scholarly face of Dr. Arabin turning in at the Deanery gate, or poor Mr. Crawley again, weak and weary with his twenty-mile walk from Hogglestock vicarage, half-starved but erect in bearing, threadbare but proud, striding toward the Palace Gates, and to that memorable interview with Mrs. Proudie. I like to fancy, too, the rival equipages of the Bishop and Archdeacon Grantly, creating a question of precedence in the narrow gateway of the Close. . . . All the shadowy souls, and many more of their shadowy friends and mine, will thrust themselves on to the peaceful lawns and elm avenues, or confront me in the quaint narrow thoroughfares leading to the Precincts, to the exclusion of those mightier and more strenuous men of old, that I ought to be thinking about, who were far from being shadows." These words will touch a tender chord in many hearts. They should bring the readers and admirers of Anthony Trollope in big battalions to Barchester—that is to Salisbury. To visit Bristol or Bath without traversing the Wiley Valley and spending a time in England's ideal cathedral city, which " the master " peopled with Proudies, Hardings, Arabins, and Grantlys, will be regarded as rank heresy by the true Trollopian. In Salisbury, at any rate, the Cathedral and the Close are still dominant factors in the fortunes of a travel-centre where you can still discover " perfect peace, unruffled calm, and a clarified, but decently drowsy, atmosphere." Salisbury is the Melchester of Thomas Hardy's novels, and its Cathedral is well known to admirers of Dickens as the building which was so constantly drawn from all points of view by the pupils of Mr. Pecksniff.

To attempt anything like a detailed description of either the exterior or the interior of Salisbury Cathedral, with its wealth of chapels, chantries, chapter-house, and cloisters, is manifestly beyond the compass of this work. " The Cathedral of Salisbury " (dedicated to the Blessed Virgin), says Thomas Fuller in his " Worthies," " is paramount in this kind, wherein the doors and chappells equall the Months, the Windows the Days, the Pillars and Pillasters of Fusill Marble (an ancient Art now suspected to be lost) the Hours of the Year, so that all Europe affords not such an Almanack of Architecture. Once walking in this Church (whereof then I was Prebendary) I met a countryman wondering at the structure thereof. ' I once,' said he to me, ' admired that there could be a Church that should have so many Pillars, as there be Hours in the Year ; and now I admire more, that there should be so many Hours in the Year, as I see Pillars in this Church.' " The architectural coincidence pointed out by Fuller, be it real or imaginary, has been thus described in verse by a Cathedral dignitary :

" *As many windows may you here behold*
As days in the revolving year are told ;
Compute the hours that one full year compose,
As many marble shafts these walls inclose,
Nor numbers Phœbus in his annual round
More months than doors within this fabric found."

Handbooks, great and small, old and new, are obtainable in abundance. All parts of the Cathedral are now open without fee to the visitor, who, as descriptions have recently been attached to the various monuments can learn much by himself ; if he desires the assistance of one of the custodians, he will find the lecture of the personally conducting verger to be distinctly in advance of the explanations vouchsafed by his official predecessors.

The few pages Mr. Bradley devotes to the subject are both informing and amusing. For him, as well as for the present verger, George III's friend, James Wyatt, the first " restorer " of the fabric, is as anathema. The man who designed the royal baths both at Windsor and Weymouth with conspicuous success wrought sad havoc and did irreparable injury at Salisbury when he began to repair the stonework of Poore, de Bridport, and de Bingham, to destroy chapels and chantries which had stood the wear and tear of centuries, to make things " neat " by the aid of whitewash, and to carry out a general rearrangement of tombs and monuments on a system of his own invention. It is on record that in the time of the Great Rebellion the Bishop's Palace was converted into an Inn, and that much damage in 1653 was done to the cloisters and the Cathedral library by the 300 Dutch prisoners who were confined there, yet the harm for which the Roundheads can be fairly held responsible is trifling in comparison to that which may justly be attributed to this overzealous eighteenth-century iconoclast, who actually pulled down bodily the mediæval belfry. Yet in an otherwise excellent guide-book published in Salisbury in 1806 we are gravely assured that " Nothing can convey a juster idea of the architect (Mr. Wyatt's) great judgment and abilities than the arrangement of the different ornaments he has selected from the chapels removed, of which the whole of this end is chiefly composed ; and their application seems very suitable to their different situations."

It must be confessed that there is some originality both in the idea of an architectural potpourri and that of a reshuffling of sepulchral effigies on the principle of the old-fashioned game known as " General Post." What was " neat and effective " as well as " right and proper " in 1806, is regarded as desecration and sacrilege in 1925. If the presence of Wyatt in Salisbury is attributable to George III, the error was in some measure atoned for by the presentation of the fine organ, which for many years stood on the stone screen which divided the Choir and Nave ; but which is now in St. Thomas's church.

Some interesting information relating to the monuments after their re-arrangement by Wyatt will be found in a handsome and elaborately illustrated work on the Cathedral, compiled by William Dodsworth (seemingly under the patronage of the Royal Family), and published in 1814. Those which always attract the attention of visitors are the recumbent figures of the pious founder Poore and his immediate predecessors and successors, with that popularly but quite erroneously assigned to a chorister or " Boy Bishop," about which so much has been written. One inscription at least finds a place in most anecdote books, but you may search in vain for any visible memorial of Mary, Countess of Pembroke, that generous patroness of poets and men of letters, who passed the last years of her useful life at Crosby Hall, lately threatened with destruction. There she died on September 25, 1621, and some days later was buried beside her husband in the tomb-house of the Herberts, beneath the pavement of the Choir in Salisbury Cathedral. Ben Jonson wrote her epitaph, and few tributes of the kind seem more likely to achieve immortality :

> " *Underneath this marble hearse*
> *Lies the subject of all verse,*
> *Sidney's sister ; Pembroke's mother ;*
> *Death ! ere thou hast slain another*
> *Wise and fair and good as she,*
> *Time shall throw a dart at thee.*"

When one reflects that William Shakespeare, who addressed his sonnets to her elder son William, refers to her in the lines :

> " *Thou art thy mother's glass and she in thee*
> *Calls back the lovely April of her prime,*"

it is certainly astonishing that the words of Jonson have never been inscribed on stone, marble, or brass near the spot where she rests.

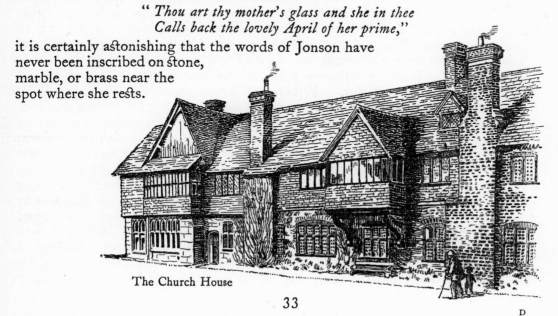

The Church House

33

D

BATH ABBEY

ATH, the "Queen City of the West," famed all the world over for its wonderful healing waters, the only hot mineral springs in Great Britain, also for its Roman remains unequalled outside Italy, as well as for its unique place in History and Literature and as the great resort of the fashionable world in the seventeenth and eighteenth centuries, is deeply interesting ecclesiastically.

The beautiful Abbey Church of Bath, commenced by Bishop King and Prior Birde in 1500, which is the central feature of the city, is authoritatively accepted as the lineal descendant of a College of Secular Canons founded by Offa, King of Mercia, A.D. 775. Some writers state that Osric, King of the Hwiccas, whose name is associated with the early stages of Gloucester Cathedral, gave to the Abbess Bertana in 676 one hundred manentes of land adjacent to the city of Bath on which to build a monastery. A charter, attested by Archbishop Theodore, relates to a further gift of land by Æthelmod, with the consent of King Ethelred, to the venerable Abbess Bernguidis and to Folcburga, the Prioress. But evidently the nuns gave place to Offa's college of secular canons, for in 758 Cynewulf, King of the West Saxons, with the assent of Offa, granted five manentes of land at North Stoke to the monks and to their monastic church of St. Peter. This church was made dependent upon Haethored, Bishop of Worcester. At a Synod in Brentford (781) Haethored returned to Offa the land granted by Cynewulf, and Bath became a royal demesne. To the church Athelstan, Edmund, and Edwy each made gifts.

The Benedictines replaced the secular canons, and in their abbey, probably a very fine church for its day, the coronation of King Edgar took place, with great pomp, on May 11, 973. The present church stands upon the site of the great Norman Cathedral (the nave of which was as large as the whole abbey to-day), built by Bishop John de Villula of Tours, chaplain and physician to William Rufus. William of Malmesbury described de Villula as "a physician qualified by practice rather than study." De Villula was professionally attracted hither by its hot springs, and, on his appointment, moved his Bishop's "stool" (1091-92) to Bath, as the largest town in his diocese. Just before Bishop John took office Robert de Mowbray devastated the church and did other great damage to the city. Villula obtained a grant of the position and revenues of the Abbot of Bath and started rebuilding. The ecclesiastical importance of Bath is shown by the fact that the Bishop was at one time "Bishop of Bath." A long struggle for supremacy was waged between the regular clergy of Bath and the secular clergy of Wells ; it was finally arranged in 1245 that the Bishop should have the title of "Bishop of Bath and Wells," and should in future be elected by delegates appointed by the monks of Bath and the canons of Wells and the title has continued ever

BATH ABBEY

BATH ABBEY: THE NAVE

since. Until 1538 the Bishop was also Abbot of Bath. Evidently there were times when the personnel of the Abbey complained of their treatment, for we find, in 1321, Bishop John of Drokensford writing that he had been informed that the wealth of the church had been so wasted by mismanagement that the brethren were not properly fed, and, further, that if one complained ever so properly the Prior threatened him with heavy punishment and even worse food.

The Abbey Church is the last complete ecclesiastical building erected before the Dissolution of the Monasteries, and gains in symmetry in being throughout of the same character (late Perpendicular) as Salisbury Cathedral is in Early English. The building, which is on the plan of a simple Latin Cross, is best seen from the north side. The remarkable height of the clerestory—there is no triforium—dwarfs what are usually the principal windows, and with the great transept and east and west windows makes the Abbey remarkable for its enormous area of glass, which has led many to call it, as also York Minster, the "Lantern of England." Its chief architectural feature is the West Front, flanked with two turrets, the sculpture upon the face of which is often called "Jacob's Ladder," as, for instance, by Sir Walter Scott, upon whose young mind it made a great impression. It is, however, the Ladder of Salvation, and illustrates a dream of Bishop Oliver King when he visited Bath in 1499, whereby he was impelled to commence the present building on the site of John de Villula's Norman Cathedral. In his dream Oliver King heard the Lord's command to build His House, and saw the angels ascending and descending from heaven discharging the ministry of the Church. In order to show that the angels were descending, the sculptor portrayed them coming down head-first. On either side of the ladders are the canopied figures of the Twelve Apostles ; and at the feet bending figures, evidently representing men in the act of adoration, with the words *De sursum est.* Over the great West window, and dominated by a figure beneath a canopy representing God the Father, are a number of carvings symbolising the Heavenly Host. The flanking buttresses contain a rebus on the name of Bishop King, and in Latin and English the following :—" Trees going to choose their King said, ' Be to us the Olive King.' " Olive leaves too are embodied in the emblems of the Passion on the spandrels of the West doors.

The visitor will be impressed by the beauty of these doors, the gift in 1616 of Sir Henry Montague, Lord Chief Justice, and brother of Bishop Montague, who was

Abbey Doorway

35

appointed to the See of Bath and Wells in 1608. The doors, now dark with age, are carved with mantles and shields bearing the arms of the Montagues and of the Bishop of Winchester.

On entering the church the visitor is inevitably impressed by its length and loftiness, and the symmetry (which was the aim of every detail in the design) of the slender piers and pointed arches with their deep mouldings, the long succession of large clerestory windows and the graceful lines of the fan-tracery vaulting, one of the glories of the Abbey. Standing beneath the lantern the visitor will notice that the East window differs from the West window in that it is square-headed and not pointed. The difference is due to its construction between the piers of the central tower of de Villula's Norman Cathedral, the bases of which are still to be seen in the east wall of the Abbey. Traces of the Norman Nave are visible in the pier on the north side of the Sanctuary, and in that at the western end of Bishop Montague's tomb. The Perpendicular window of the War Memorial Chapel in the south choir aisle is built inside a Norman arch, while a cluster of Norman pillars and the old floor of the Cathedral—which was seven feet lower than the floor of the Abbey—are to be found beneath a grating at the east end of the north aisle. In the south wall near the entrance to the War Memorial Chapel is a doorway which led at one time to the Cloisters, while on the same side near the Font is the old Prior's doorway.

The visitor will be attracted to the only Chantry chapel—that of Prior William Birde (1499–1525) who (says " The Original Bath Guide ") " warmly and generously seconded Bishop Oliver King in building the church whereupon he ' expended so much of his own means that he died poor,' and like it, his chapel was left unfinished." Few Chantry chapels are in a finer state of preservation than this, which in its way is a gem with exquisite stone carving and fan-traceried roof. The Prior's rebus appears in the tracery. The carving is worth close examination, particularly the undercut work with the chisel, and the delicate fashioning of the birds and clusters of grapes, so minute as to give the appearance of having been cut from ivory rather than out of stone. In the course of time, the beautiful Chantry suffered damage. The whitewash with which it was covered was removed in 1833 by Mr. Edward Davis, an architect of Bath, who skilfully repaired the stonework. Finally the carving was completed at the expense of the Kemble family.

The East end of the Abbey from the eastern side of the Lantern was completed in the year 1522. The vaulting of the Choir, 76 feet above the floor, of entrancing beauty, has been truly likened " to the interlacing branches of giant palms in a tropical forest." The scheme of vaulting was faithfully adopted for the remainder of the Abbey by Sir Gilbert Scott in the great restoration work which he carried out on the initiative of the Rev. Charles Kemble, Rector of Bath from 1859 until his death in 1874, to whom the city of Bath and the Abbey owes much. The vaulting certainly ranks amongst the finest there is in Great Britain, and to its beauty, and that of the slender piers and pointed arches, the rich light from the Clerestory windows lends much charm.

The walls are crowded with monuments to honoured names of the seventeenth and eighteenth centuries, when the Abbey was a favourite place of burial. " There's snug lying in the Abbey," wrote Richard Brinsley Sheridan. A fine piece of work is that by Roubiliac, " The Good Samaritan " dedicated to Jacob Bosanquet (*d.* 1767). The epitaphs, some of them curiously worded and others by prominent writers of their day, will retain the visitor's attention for some time. Bishop Montague, to whom reference has already been made, and who became Bishop of Winchester, was at his own request buried in Bath Abbey, the alabaster and black marble monument on the north side of the Nave being erected to his memory by his brothers. On the south side of the Choir aisle will be seen a list of the Abbesses, Abbots, Priors and Rectors of Bath, commencing with Bertana (A.D. 676) and Bernguidis (A.D. 681), and in reading this list one will recall that among the rulers of the monastery at Bath were famous men, to name only one, St. Alphege, who, according to *The Golden Legend*, became a monk at Deerhurst, five miles from Gloucester : " And when St. Alphege had been monk there a long time living a full holy life, then he went from thence to the Abbey of Bath to be there in more contemplation and rest of soul. . . . He led there a full holy life, and much well he guided the monks in holy and virtuous living." St. Alphege, who became Archbishop of Canterbury, was murdered by the Danes at Greenwich in 1014.

The Abbey is in every way worthy of the ancient city, of which it has been said " A Queen of the West she reigneth alone."

BRISTOL CATHEDRAL

Oh ! hadde I now a mockeler poyntell,
Muche sholde I lacke in wordies now to sayne,
Fitzhardynge's gloryous dedes and workes to telle ;
The mynster speketh here, battaunte and plaine !

Staie, faytore, staie, these bawson pillarrs kenn ;
Awhope thie Ee wythe cloude-hylt Towyrs hyghe,
Buylte bie Fitzhardynge, firste of all mortale men,
Whose fayme wyl sheen for aye and neyr die !

Ancient MS.

BRISTOL, on account of its wealth of ecclesiastical architecture, recalls to mind continental cities, on great rivers
or near the sea, which owe their beautiful churches mainly
to great families and the merchant princes of bygone days.
Bristol is chiefly indebted for its churches to some great
baronial houses—the Earls of Gloucester and the Berkeleys—
and to such men of commerce as William Canynges, the
Shipwards, and the Framptons.

The Cathedral at Bristol will repay careful attention, although it is not
so large as Salisbury or Exeter. It began its existence as the church of an
Abbey of Augustinian, or Black, Canons as far back as 1142. That abbey
was built by Robert Fitzharding, a burgess of Bristol, descended from the
Kings of Denmark, and founder of the Berkeley family. His descendants
still reign at Berkeley Castle. Dugdale, in his "Monasticon Anglicanum,"
describes Fitzharding as a rich citizen of Bristol who " was so much in favour
of Henry II that he gave him the barony of Berchale and all Berchaleiness
with all the Churches, etc., and he also gave all these churches to the Canons
of St. Augustine at Bristol. The charter of Edward II recites that of Henry,
Duke of Normandy, afterwards King of England, and both of them enumerate
and confirm the several donations made to these canons." At the time of
the erection of Fitzharding's monastery Henry was being educated at Bristol.
The inscription over the Great Norman Gateway, which is one of the few
portions of the monastery still extant, shows Henry's interest in the building,
which that monarch, from his early boyhood, encouraged by a number of gifts.
The consecration of the church as an Augustinian Abbey took place on Easter
Day, 1148, in the presence of the Bishops of Worcester, Exeter, St. Asaph,
and Llandaff.

After the Dissolution of the Monasteries, Bristol became an episcopal See
with the Abbey Church as its Cathedral in 1542. Dugdale writes caustically :
" When King Henry VIII had robbed the Church of infinite treasure by

38

BRISTOL CATHEDRAL

Copyright: Victor H. Tarl

BRISTOL CATHEDRAL: CHOIR

Facing page 39

suppression of all the Monasteries throughout England, the better to palliate the Sacrilege he made show of refunding some part thereof by erecting six new bishopricks including that of Bristol." The Abbey Church of St. Augustine was selected as Bristol's cathedral, though, " like other things ordered in that confusion," Heylin observed that the diocese—the County of Dorset— was far distant from its cathedral city.

The first Bishop of Bristol was Paul Bush, whose writings show him to have been learned in medicine as well as divinity. Consecrated in 1542, he was deprived of his office by Queen Mary " for being marry'd." For over thirty years in the reign of Elizabeth, Bristol was without a bishop, and " was on the whole held *in commendam* by the Bishops of Gloucester, during which time the patrimony of the Church was much wasted." Since that time the See of Bristol has played an important part in the ecclesiastical affairs of the Nation, particularly in the West of England.

Before the Dissolution, the Abbey Church had fallen into such decay that it became necessary to remove the Norman Nave. It however contains a number of architectural features of more than ordinary interest. The Abbey Gateway leading into College Green conveys by its stateliness and richly sculptured mouldings an idea of the character of the work for which Fitz-harding's monastic church was famous. The Chapter House and vestibule, which with the gateway and other smaller features comprise all that remains of the Norman Church, are really very beautiful, strikingly rich in detail. This Chapter House, one of the finest specimens of Norman work in the United Kingdom, was mutilated in the eighteenth century, and again during the Reform Riots of 1831, when damage amounting to over £200,000 was done in the city. The Vestibule is remarkable for the combination of round and pointed arches ; the bases of the columns were restored to view in 1923.

One of the outstanding features of the Cathedral is the Early English " elder " Lady Chapel—so called to distinguish it from the later chapel with the same dedication, at the East End. It was erected between 1215 and 1234 by Abbot David, who was buried therein. The curious carvings should be noted.

The central tower, which was a feature of the Norman Church, was rebuilt later in the Perpendicular style, and conspicuous among its decorations is the white rose of York.

The Choir, which replaced the Norman Choir in 1306, consists of five bays—the Choir Screen, Sedilia, and Reredos being good modern work, the stalls carefully renewed with the ancient misericords beneath. The Eastern Lady Chapel lies beyond, and all this belongs to the Early or Geometrical Period, and is the work principally of Abbot Knowle. The splendid coloured glass of the great East Window " like an inestimable treasure of precious stones, and with all its brilliancy as soft as rose leaves," is considered to be amongst the finest in England, dating mostly from 1320. The symbolical arrange-ment of the window and the division of the Reredos beneath it into three parts serves to remind the visitor of the fact that the church was rededicated to the

Holy Trinity. According to Horace Walpole the enamelled windows on the east of the Choir aisles were given by Nell Gwynne. Leading into the Berkeley Chapel is a unique Sacristy. The canopied tombs of the Berkeleys with effigies in coats of mail, and the recumbent figures of the mitred and croziered Abbots should be examined. There is also a wonderful sculpture of Anglo-Saxon date of the "harrowing of hell" in the South Transept; while the Newton Chapel adjoining has a remarkable altar tomb. The present Nave, which was completed in 1877, accords with the style of the Choir. Fragments of a carved stone screen, incorporated in the back of the Sedilia, include the arms of Edward VI when Prince of Wales. The tombs in the Cathedral include those of the Abbots and Bishop Bush, while others commemorated are Bishop Butler, the famous theologian, who was for twelve years Bishop of Bristol, Robert Southey, who was a native of Bristol, and Edward Colston, merchant and philanthropist. In an excellent "Harrowing of Hell" short summary of the growth and principal features of Bristol Cathedral the Dean (the Very Rev. E. A. Burroughs) places on record the following letter written to Mr. Osmond in 1833 by Mr. Augustus Welby N. Pugin, one of the great leaders of the Gothic revival in English architecture who was called in by Barry to prepare the drawings for the Houses of Parliament : " While at Bristol I paid particular attention to the Cathedral, in which I find many things deserving most particular attention. This Cathedral has been generally overlooked as undeserving of notice, but the fact is that there are parts about it equal to anything in the country. The groins of the aisles, the carving in part of the stalls, the vestry (*i.e.* Sacristy), the tombs in the aisles round the choir, the great east window, the Norman entrance to the Chapter House from the Cloisters, are all most interesting, and to real Gothic men, like you and me, it affords a great treat. The east window is so truly beautiful that I have just marked out the tracing of it for you. The original glass is still in it, and the effect is wonderfully rich and varied."

A recent survey of the Cathedral revealed the urgent necessity for certain repairs, including the underpinning of the East Cloister. New vestries have been erected on the site of part of the original monastic buildings, the actual foundations of which have been utilised ; the Consistory Court has been transferred and an ancient passage opened up connecting the vestries of the Dean and Canons with the church. The Cathedral of Bristol occupies a worthy place amongst the greater churches of our country.

No visitor with a love of archæology and sense of the beautiful will leave the city of Bristol without having paid a visit to St. Mary Redcliffe Church, designated by Leland, who professed to have seen every edifice in England, as " by far the fairest of all churches," and the assertion was reiterated by Camden, while good Queen Bess declared it to be " the goodliest and most famous parish church in England." St. Mary Redcliffe is in fact considered to be the finest parish church in Europe, with only St. Ouen in Rouen as a possible rival. It is apparently the third which has stood on the same site, for traces have been discovered of a Romanesque church, and there are important remains—notably in the tower and the inner north porch—of the thirteenth-century building by which this was succeeded. The site was admirably chosen—a natural terrace of the sandstone, which gives its name to the locality dominating the busy river which flows at its feet and the low-lying plain on which ancient Bristol stands.

Very little is actually known of the first and second churches which stood upon this site. Unfortunately the archives suffered through many documents, which might have thrown some light on the history of the site, being destroyed by Thomas Chatterton, the "Marvellous Boy" poet, and his father, who had access to the ancient chests in the Muniment Room over the North Porch. The Domesday Book contains no mention of a church at Redcliffe, although, as stated above, traces of a Romanesque edifice have been discovered. The reference to a church in a charter of Henry II (1158) confirming endowments of the churches at Bedminster and Redcliffe to Salisbury Cathedral probably relates to this edifice. One of the signatories to a deed concerning a chapel at Bishopsworth (*circa* 1189) was William, Chaplain of Redcliffe. Another charter (1232) refers to the bell tower of Redcliffe. It is known that in 1247 relaxations of penances were granted to all who "devoutly visit the Church of the Blessed Mary of Radclive and there charitably contribute to the repair of the same."

Between 1327 and 1389 much of the second church was pulled down and the present wonderful building was begun, the first portions undertaken being the South Transept, South Porch, and South Nave aisle.

Some portions of the funds for this church were provided by William Canynges, the grandfather of one of the merchant princes of the middle of the fifteenth century, who himself made munificent contributions towards the completion of St. Mary's, including the raising of the vault to 54 feet, the extension of the Lady Chapel, the substitution of large windows for the small clerestory lights, etc. Some 100 masons and carpenters were employed by the later William Canynges "to repair and edify, cover and glaze the Church of Redcliffe." Singularly enough, there are two effigies of this fifteenth-century benefactor: one close to a similarly recessed effigy of his wife, in a stellated recess in the south aisle ; the other in the south transept, representing him as a priest, is considered to have been brought from the collegiate church of Westbury, of which he became dean shortly before his death in 1474. Other noteworthy memorials are those

Muniment Room

41

of a mailed warrior (*circa* 1220), supposed to represent a Berkeley, which must have originally lain in the Norman church; a rich altar tomb of the Mede family (*circa* 1475); a figure known as "Canynges almoner"; another of a priest (*circa* 1393); and a monument to the memory of Admiral Sir William Penn, father of the celebrated Quaker who founded Pennsylvania, and a native of the city. Admiral Sir William Penn commanded the fleet at the capture of Jamaica, 1655. In January 1914 the Bishop of Bristol dedicated a window erected in the south transept "in pious memory of the men who made Bristol famous in the fourteenth and fifteenth centuries." Twelve Bristol worthies are thus commemorated. There are also some good brasses.

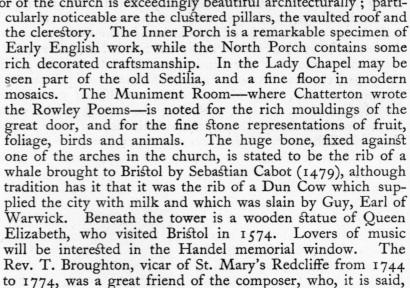

Penn Monument

The architectural features of St. Mary's may be divided as follows: Early English period (1190–1270)—the Inner North Porch, the lower portion of the Tower, a corbel on the south face of the Tower in the Nave; Decorated Period (1270–1370)—the South Transept, South Aisle and South Porch walls, the lower portion of the spire and the upper section of the Tower, and the Hexagonal North Porch; Late Decorated and Perpendicular Period (1370–1520)—the clerestory windows, North Transept and part of South Porch, South Aisle windows and vaulting; the stone vault and flat roof, etc. The interior of the church is exceedingly beautiful architecturally; particularly noticeable are the clustered pillars, the vaulted roof and the clerestory. The Inner Porch is a remarkable specimen of Early English work, while the North Porch contains some rich decorated craftsmanship. In the Lady Chapel may be seen part of the old Sedilia, and a fine floor in modern mosaics. The Muniment Room—where Chatterton wrote the Rowley Poems—is noted for the rich mouldings of the great door, and for the fine stone representations of fruit, foliage, birds and animals. The huge bone, fixed against one of the arches in the church, is stated to be the rib of a whale brought to Bristol by Sebastian Cabot (1479), although tradition has it that it was the rib of a Dun Cow which supplied the city with milk and which was slain by Guy, Earl of Warwick. Beneath the tower is a wooden statue of Queen Elizabeth, who visited Bristol in 1574. Lovers of music will be interested in the Handel memorial window. The Rev. T. Broughton, vicar of St. Mary's Redcliffe from 1744 to 1774, was a great friend of the composer, who, it is said, revised some of his oratorios in the church. The visitor will feel it difficult to leave St. Mary's, of which Chatterton wrote

"Thou seest this maystrie of a human hand,
The pride of Brystowe and the Westerne Land."

42

ST. MARY REDCLIFFE (BRISTOL)

ST. MARY REDCLIFFE: THE NORTH AISLE

Facing page 43

In the churchyard stands a monument to Chatterton, who was born, and lived for nearly all his short life, within the shadow of St. Mary's. On the south side has been erected as a war memorial a replica of the old Preaching Cross, where four sermons were delivered on Good Friday, Easter Day, and Monday and Tuesday of Easter Week.

Lovers of old-world treasures will find themselves pre-eminently at home in "Busy Bristol." There are such buildings as St. Peter's Hospital, the Merchant Venturers' Hall, and the Seamen's Almshouses. No visitor should ever leave Bristol, whose proud device ever since 1567 has been "Valour and Industry," without seeing them. Close to the Almshouses is the City Library, founded by Robert Redwood in 1613, the pioneer of the Free Library system of which, as far as Bristol is concerned, it is now the centre. Grinling Gibbons carved the monumental mantel-piece, and many and priceless are the rarities in its well-filled book-shelves.

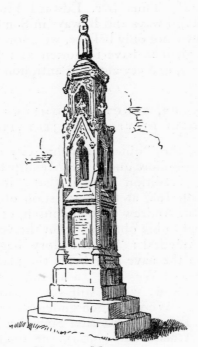

Chatterton Monument

WELLS CATHEDRAL

HERE are few places in the whole of the British Isles more fascinating both to the antiquary and to the ecclesiologist than Wells—the City of Many Streams, the Wellys or Ad Fontes of our forefathers—the English Bruges, where a moat still encircles the Bishop's Palace, and nearly everything which meets the eye savours of an order of things which vanished at the Reformation. The tone of Wells is, and always has been, essentially theological. Peace prevailed within its precincts almost without a break, until a summer day in A.D. 1685, when Monmouth's soldiers stabled their horses in the Cathedral Nave, and would have proceeded to further enormities but for the timely intervention of Lord Grey. It was as far back as A.D. 705 that the first church of Wells, with its subordinate college of secular priests, was founded. Wells therefore might have celebrated its millenary in Queen Anne's reign, but apparently missed the opportunity. The verb " to pag " was not then added to the English dictionary. A Roman settlement existed at Wells.

" There are places in the world so beautiful, so happy or so sacred, that to speak of them now without a certain reverent hesitation might seem impossible ; of these Wells is one." Thus Mr. Edward Hutton heads his delightful chapter on Wells in " Highways and Byways in Somerset " (Macmillan & Co., London). " In Wells we not only believe, we know and we feel, that men have been happy . . . though men have forgotten and been silent so long, those towers still sing *Te Deum*, and cry aloud in antiphon with the hills out of which they were hewn :

SANCTUS, SANCTUS, SANCTUS, DOMINUS DEUS SABAOTH ;
PLENI SUNT COELI ET TERRA MAJESTATIS GLORIAE TUAE."

As its name shows, the " quiet Cathedral city of poetic imagination," so charmingly situated in a hollow under the Mendip Hills, is a place of springs, wells, and fountains. Tradition gives it that " it was precisely because of those waters " that King Ina, at the suggestion of St. Aldhelm in A.D. 705, built to the honour of St. Andrew a small church, of which nothing remains.

The excellent official guide obtained from the vergers gives a brief historical account of the Cathedral : " Our history begins 1200 years ago. A stone near the pulpit in the nave now holds the place of an earlier one which commemorated King Ina of Wessex. In his days, if not before, a church rose by the wells of St. Andrew, which still spring abundantly in the Bishop's garden and fill his moat. We were then under the rule of the famous Aldhelm, bishop of Sherborne. Two centuries later Somerset became a separate diocese. Our first bishop was Athelm (*circa* 909), the uncle of St. Dunstan. Both became archbishops of Canterbury : the uncle crowned King Athelstan, the

WELLS CATHEDRAL: THE WEST FRONT

WELLS CATHEDRAL

nephew crowned King Edgar. A notable figure in our history is Giso of Lorraine, one of those able foreigners whom Edward the Confessor brought over, and who helped to prepare the way, though all unconsciously, for the Norman settlement. Sent on a mission from the King to the Pope, he was consecrated at Rome in A.D. 1061. We still possess the Bull which he brought home confirming him in his see. Giso erected a cloister for the canons of Wells, and made them live together after the foreign manner. He retained his see through the reign of the Conqueror, and died in 1088. Then John of Tours, his successor, broke up Giso's establishment at Wells, and making himself abbot of Bath, changed his title from Bishop of Wells to Bishop of Bath. Half a century later Bishop Robert, in King Stephen's time, reorganised the canons of Wells and repaired or rebuilt their church. He instituted a dean, precentor, chancellor, and treasurer, after the manner of Bishop Osmund of Salisbury, and endowed some twenty prebends. Of his church hardly more than one stone remains. The date of the present church is a problem in English architecture. Our historians, guided by documents, have been led to assign to Bishop Reginald, who died in 1191, the western bays of the choir, the two transepts and the eastern bays of the nave. It is certain that the work had well begun in his time : more than this cannot safely be said."

Reginald de Bohun's work was continued by Bishops Savary (1192–1205), Jocelin (1206–42), and William de Marchia (1293–1302), and by Dean John de Godelee (1306–33). Jocelin of Wells, a brother of Bishop Hugh II of Lincoln, was one of the bishops who were at the side of Stephen Langton at the signing of Magna Charta. In many ways he was exceptionally active, his building work including the glorious West front of the Cathedral, the bishop's palace, a choristers' school, grammar school, hospital for travellers, and a chapel and manor house at Wookey, two miles from Wells. This work stands as that of one of the three " master builders of our holy and beautiful house of St. Andrew in Wells." Associated with Jocelin was Elias of Dereham, a famous designer who died in 1246.

Jocelin's West front—Flaxman styled it " A masterpiece of Art indeed. . . . England affordeth not the like "—flanked on either side by two towers, the upper parts of which are in Perpendicular style, contains no less than nine tiers of undamaged sculpture, with about 300 figures, nearly all of heroic proportions, some as much as eight feet in height. In addition there are smaller statues of angels, saints and prophets, kings and queens of England, bishops and benefactors to the Cathedral, and forty-eight reliefs of Biblical subjects, with large representations of the Resurrection (containing about 150 figures) and the Last Judgment. " What the ancient glory of that mighty frontal must have been," says Mr. Hutton, " when it was covered with silver and gold, with scarlet and purple and blue, and the beauty of all colours, we cannot perhaps realise. It must have been like a page from some glorious Book of Hours ; yet when on a fortunate evening the sun falls upon it until sunset, it shines, even now, with so great and dazzling a splendour that I have thought to see there that work of praise and worship as it was when new from Bishop

Jocelin's hands. There can have been nothing like it in England, nor perhaps in the world ; though it was done with a knowledge of the still earlier work at Amiens and Chartres, in size and in splendour and unity it surpassed them both, and it is perhaps needless to say that there is nothing comparable to it left upon earth." Mr. Hutton thinks the idea of the whole may be more fully understood by turning to the account of the Death, Assumption and Coronation of the Blessed Virgin as given in " The Golden Legend " of Jacobus de Voragine, in which is told how at her death all the Apostles were gathered about her, and " at the third hour of the night came Christ with sweet melody, with the Orders of Angels, the Company of Patriarchs, the Assemblies of Martyrs, the Covenants of Confessors, the Carols of Virgins in order and with sweet song and melody."

Canon Church gives a different rendering of the great frontal. " Here," he writes, " as men laid their dead to rest, they might look up and see and read this ' Sermon in stones,' telling in one tier of sculptures the story of man's creation and his fall ; his redemption and his resurrection to life. In another tier they might see the commemoration of the faithful departed, kings and 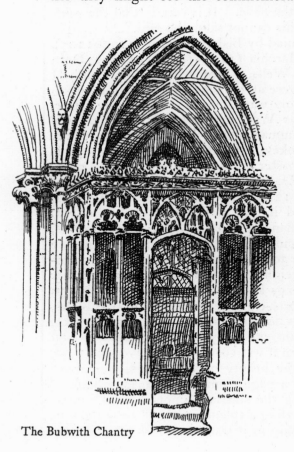 bishops, mailed warriors, and ministers of the sanctuary ; queens and holy women, types of the honourable of the Earth who had served God standing in their places in life. And then higher up, these are seen rising from their graves on the Resurrection morning to stand before the company of Heaven, angels and archangels and the Twelve Apostles of the Lamb, and before the Son of Man seated on His throne, ' high and lifted up ' above all, for judgment. Faintly now can we imagine the impressive dignity and glory of this sculptured front as the western sun glowed upon these stately figures, some of matchless grace, as they stood out from under the canopies of their niches, the shadows in the background darkened by artistic colouring. . . . We are here in presence of one of the monumental records of man's genius and art, mysterious in its origin, telling a story in stone of the Unseen World, such as Dante sang in undying verse later in that century which produced this creation in our midst."

The central tower, which rises to a height of 160 feet, was continued in

The Bubwith Chantry

46

WELLS CATHEDRAL: THE NAVE

WELLS CATHEDRAL: STEPS TO CHAPTER HOUSE

A.D. 1318, having been carried in earlier years only up to the level of the roof. Some years afterwards, however, it was found that the four massive piers were sinking and were insufficient to carry the weight of the tower. The catastrophe was averted with remarkable skill by the mediæval builders, who placed inverted arches on three sides under the lantern, thus supporting the piers from top to bottom. The whole work, which Glastonbury copied later, was accomplished with graceful effect. The south tower was not begun until after A.D. 1386 ; the north tower, begun in A.D. 1424, presents some slight difference of detail.

Under three deans, Walter Haselshaw (1295–1302), Henry Husee (1302–1305) and John Godelee (1305–33), considerable enlargement took place. The Choir was lengthened, a new Lady Chapel built, and two eastern transepts, while the Chapter House was another important addition.

The Choir contains an elaborate figure of Bishop Ralph of Shrewsbury, who came to Wells in 1329, when the Choir and Lady Chapel were approaching completion. Over the High Altar is the Golden Window, an excellent example of fourteenth-century work. The window, like the Jesse Window now in St. Mary's Church, Shrewsbury, shows the reclining figure of Jesse, from whom springs the Vine, with branches and tendrils enclosing representatives of the line of David. In the centre is the Blessed Virgin, and, immediately above, Christ on the Cross. In niches below the window are figures of Our Saviour, St. Peter and St. Andrew, St. Dunstan and St. Patrick (the gifts of an anonymous benefactor), and St. David and St. George given by Somerset Freemasons in memory of members of that fraternity who fell in the war. The three bays of the Choir east of the magnificent fifteenth-century Bishop's throne form the Presbytery built in the fourteenth century, while the three western bays belong to the original building, and are the oldest part of the existing Cathedral. The Misericord seats, of which there are sixty in the Choir, are finely carved, combining, says Canon Church, " with the early semi-Norman sculpture and the grotesque capitals in the nave and transepts, and with the figures and imagery in stone on the western front, to complete a continuous series of mediæval carving remarkable for the blending of grim humour and playfulness, loving study of homely and natural subjects, with grave dignity and mysterious meaning."

The Lady Chapel, a very rich piece of decorated work, with a semi-octagonal appearance, forms with the Transitional bays, which connect it with the Choir, what is considered to be the finest eastern end of any Cathedral in this country. Professor E. A. Freeman wrote of the Chapel : " With the exquisite beauty of the Lady Chapel everyone is familiar ; but everyone may not have remarked how distinct it is from the rest of the Church : it would stand perfectly well by itself as a detached building. As it is it gives an apsidal form to the extreme end of the Church : but it is much more than an apse ; it is in fact an octagon no less than the Chapter House, and to its form it owes much of its beauty." To quote Mr. Hutton again (who describes the Chapel as " a thing beyond criticism or praise, an immortal and perfect loveliness ") : " Here, at Wells, the usual English east end, square and blunt, lacking in fancy and imagination as many have thought, is magically avoided, and all that the subtle French builder achieved with his apsidal chapels is suddenly won by a

Famous " Quarter Jack " Clock

stroke of genius for this English church, but in a simpler fashion." Mr. Francis Bond says the " putting up of an outer ring of four more piers round the western part of the octagon of the Lady Chapel was an intuition of Genius ; it makes the vistas into the Retro-choir and Lady Chapel a veritable glimpse into fairy land; and provides here alone in England a rival to the glorious eastern terminations of Amiens and Le Mans."

Of the excellently proportioned Nave it has been said " there is no nave in which the eye is so irresistibly carried eastward as in that of Wells." Superbly clustered pillars divide it into ten bays, the capitals of each pillar being dexterously and quaintly carved. One capital shows a shoemaker, another a fruit stealer, another a fox with a goose, and another a man with the toothache. Between the second and third piers on the north side of the Nave is the Bubwith Chantry, noteworthy for its cornices and screen work, a beautiful Perpendicular chapel. Opposite is the chantry built for Hugh Sugar, Treasurer of Wells (A.D. 1460–89). In the north transept is the famous " Quarter Jack " clock in which the device of a tournament used for recording the hours is not the least of its many quaint features. At the striking of the hours a company of four mounted men armed with lances conduct a mimic tourney upon a little platform over the dial, and a seated figure in knee-breeches kicks a bell at each quarter of an hour. The quarters are sounded outside by two knights in fifteenth-century armour with battle-axes.

The Chapter House, which is reached by a wonderful staircase from the north Choir aisle, is unsurpassed in beauty. The windows, with their delicate tracery, contain fragments of the original glass. Like the Lady Chapel, it is incomparable for its vaulting. " It was," wrote Mr. Francis Bond, " in the west of England that the art of Gothic vaulting was first mastered, and it was in the west, first apparently at Wells, that every arch was pointed, and the semi-circular arch exterminated."

The Cloisters, which measure 160 by 150 feet, lie to the south of the Nave. The style of the Cloisters, its outer walls and south-east door belongs to the thirteenth century. The present eastern

Jack Blandiver

48

arcade above which is the Library, was built in Bishop Bubwith's time ; the western arcade, with the Audit Room and the Song School over it, was built by Bishop Beckington (A.D. 1443–65). In the cemetery east of the Cloisters stood another Lady Chapel, which was rebuilt by Bishop Stillington about A.D. 1490, and was destroyed in A.D. 1553. This was the only serious loss which the fabric of the church suffered in those perilous days.

Next in interest is the Bishop's Palace. Its crenellated walls, gateway, and moat were erected in A.D. 1343. Inside the grounds are the ruins of the Banqueting Hall, dismantled in A.D. 1555—the largest in England, with the exception of Westminster Hall.

Vicars' Close, with its fifty small houses forming the most perfect Gothic thoroughfare in England, was originally built as the College of Singing Clerks of the Cathedral. Here time seems to have stood still ever since Bishop Ralph of Shrewsbury designed the Close in the middle of the fourteenth century. The visitor to Wells will also be attracted by the graceful and unique Chain Gate spanning the Bath Road, and the ingeniously contrived Water Conduit, for both of which Wells is indebted to Bishop Beckington, and the glorious Parish Church of St. Cuthbert, one of those splendid Perpendicular buildings known in Somerset as "Quarter Cathedrals." It is only from Tor Hill, after having visited St. Andrew's Church itself, that the surpassing loveliness of the noble Cathedral, which has been aptly described as "a precious jewel set in an emerald landscape," can be realised. The rocky crests and tree-clad sides of the Mendips provide an ideal background for the peaceful scene, while, looking westwards, the far-reaching prospect, across moorlands, meadows, coppices, and hedgerows, is bounded only by the waters of the Severn Sea.

The Chain Gate

EXETER CATHEDRAL

OVER thirteen hundred years ago in a monastery which stood on what are now the precincts of Exeter Cathedral, Boniface, English Saint and Apostle of Germany, a son of Devon, was educated under Abbot Wolphard. To the Monastery Athelstan gave many gifts, and rebuilt the church. There is good authority for believing that it was dedicated to the Blessed Virgin Mary and St. Peter. Benedictine monks, who were installed in the monastery, left it for fear of the Danes who destroyed the building more than once. Edward the Confessor transferred the See of Devon from Crediton to Exeter A.D. 1050, and installed Leofric as first Bishop of Exeter, the conventual church of the monastery becoming the cathedral church.

In a glass case in the Cathedral Library may be seen what is claimed by some to be Edward the Confessor's Charter, by virtue of which the bishop's seat or "stool" was removed from Crediton. It bears the names of the King, of Earl Godwin, of Harold (afterwards king) who fell at Hastings, of Tostig, of the two Archbishops, of Stigand, of half-a-dozen bishops and abbots, and an equal number of bishops and thanes. Sir W. Hope, however, says : " This deed is only a thirteenth Century copy (or " forgery ") of something and does not bear a single original mark or signature." There is a copy bound up with Bishop Bronescombe's register and also in that of Bishop Brantyngham, but these are not identical.

" Nowhere," wrote the late Chancellor Edmonds, " is there a cathedral of greater originality, of more complete harmony, or more obvious and striking unity." According to Professor Freeman, " the Cathedral forms a class of itself. As far as details go, no building of its age shews us the taste of that age in greater perfection." Chancellor Edmonds contends with much reason that Exeter Cathedral " does not hold its high place in the hierarchy of churches in virtue of the area of ground which it covers. It does not rank in magnitude with the great cathedral of Wessex, or the greater church of Canterbury, or with Lincoln, or with York, but in originality in harmony, in unity, it bears comparison with the proudest of them all." Such was also the opinion of the late Archbishop Temple the fourth son of Devon since the Reformation to guide the destinies of the Shire of the Sea Kings in matters ecclesiastical. Sir Francis Fox, the eminent authority, whose work for the preservation of our ancient cathedrals is widely recognised, says : " Exeter is one of the smaller but most beautiful of minsters of England."

Of the Saxon church, which Leofric used as his cathedral, only a few fragments now remain above ground. Doubtless it was greatly inferior to the Norman edifice which Bishop Warelwast, nephew of the Conqueror (1107–36), commenced to build to the west of it in 1112. Apparently a century was spent on the work, which was finished by Bishop Marshall (1194–1206) according to the plan and foundation of his predecessors.

EXETER CATHEDRAL: THE WEST FRONT

EXETER CATHEDRAL: REAR VIEW

It is, however, to Bishop Bronescombe that we owe much of the grandeur of St. Peter's, a cathedral unsurpassed in richness of detail. Quivil, his successor and friend, carried on the work and his was a bold step to insert arches and then remove the inner walls of the two massive towers (unique, except for a copy in the collegiate church at Ottery St. Mary) erected by Warelwast and to open out the north and south transepts, inserting large windows. Quivil lies buried in the Lady Chapel.

The building was continued under Bronescombe's successors. Bishop Grandisson (1327–69) survived to complete the Nave, which is 350 feet in length. The stonework of Grandisson's windows is considered to be the best example of the fine work of the period. Grandisson's master craftsmen designed and began to build the magnificent screen which is the glory of the west front. This beautiful façade, with its sculptured figures, was probably finished by Bishop Brantyngham (1370–94), to whom credit is given for the Great East Window.

Little work was done during the succeeding episcopates in the times of the great religious and political events which characterised the reigns of Henry VIII, Edward VI, Mary, Elizabeth, and Charles I, whose child Henrietta, destined to figure prominently in the regime of Louis XIV, was born and baptised at Exeter. The present font dates from this time.

During the Commonwealth the Cathedral was divided by a brick wall erected upon the organ screen and blocking also the entrances to the choir aisles. At the Restoration this wall was pulled down, and Bishop Seth Ward (1662–67) effected many alterations. Thenceforward no work of importance was done to the Cathedral until early in the nineteenth century, when important, but objectionable, restoration was done under Kendall. Yet again the whole of the interior was restored in 1870–77, under the superintendance of the late Sir G. G. Scott, at a cost of £40,000.

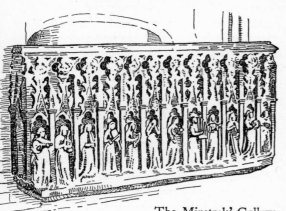

The Minstrels' Gallery

Within the glorious edifice the pilgrim should take his stand with his back to the Great West Window. Looking eastward, the magnificent *coup d'œil* is complete. One realises the exquisite beauty of the graceful roof vaulting, and the completeness of that delightful harmony of detail. The symmetry of the architecture and the dual beauty of the building is apparent in glancing down the grand vista formed by the thirty columns of Purbeck marble—a vista " not broken by the lofty organ, behind which are seen glimpses of the silvery colouring of the Eastern Window." The rich and varied tracery of the windows demands special attention ; no two similar windows will be found side by side, but only in opposite pairs.

Immediately to the right of the Great West Window, over the north-west entrance, is a window to the memory of Richard Blackmore (the author of " Lorna Doone "), an excellent portrait of whom is on a mural tablet immediately under it. In the North Porch are the fragments of a Calvary, with a cleverly executed *Agnus Dei*.

The far-famed and unrivalled Minstrel's Gallery, built in the north clerestory by Grandisson about 1360, shows twelve angels " playing on instruments of musick," which have been identified as the clarion, the cittern, the bagpipe, the rebec, the sackbut, the syrinx, the regals, the psaltery, the shawm, the gittern, the timbrel, and the cymbals. The Gallery occupies the central bay over the Nave arches. The richly sculptured Pulpit, composed entirely of Mansfield stone, was erected in 1877 to the memory of John Patteson, D.D., Bishop of Melanesia, who was killed at Nukapu in the South Pacific Ocean.

The lovely stone Choir screen, *circa* 1324, the gift of Bishop Stapeldon, has paintings of a later date describing Biblical events, from the Creation to the Pentecost. The arches of this screen were pierced on either side in the restoration of the Cathedral (1870–77). The central arch forms the entrance into the Choir, the richly gilded iron gates of which are popularly known as the " Golden Gates." The Choir is exquisitely beautiful, the stalls being of close-grained oak, canopied and pinnacled, and covered with minute and elaborate carvings. The ancient misereres are worth close examination. The splendid East Window is early Perpendicular, and differs from every other window in the Cathedral. The ancient stained glass is one of the finest examples of mediæval work.

The Nave aisles are filled with a rich and varied number of monuments—mural tablets in marble and bronze—which will prove of great interest to the visitor. In the north transept is a clock, reputed to have been made by Peter Lightfoot, the monk of Glastonbury responsible for the fine specimen of clock-making at Wimborne Minster. Beneath this marvellous contrivance is the inscription *Pereunt et imputantur*, " They (the hours) pass and are placed to our account."

The noble fane strikes the eye from most of the approaches to the City. The best nearer view is obtained from the Broadgate, the principal entrance to " The Close." From this point the visitor gains a fine impression of the magnificent west front, and rising through the elm trees in the beautiful " Green " is the massive square north tower, with the north-western side of the Cathedral.

Carvings on the West Front

EXETER CATHEDRAL: THE NAVE

EXETER CATHEDRAL: THE CHOIR

But nowhere can the strong individual exterior be seen to greater advantage than from the garden of the Bishop's Palace, which lies to the south and south-east. Here the pilgrims have a picturesque view of the south tower, the Lady Chapel, the tracery of the windows, and the flying buttresses supporting the Choir. The citizens of Exeter have a deep-seated love for their beautiful Cathedral, a love which was exemplified in tangible form when the Mayor handed the Dean a cheque for £10,000, the sum realised as the result of an appeal made by the Mayor during Lent, for the Exeter Cathedral Restoration Fund. The gift exceeded by £2,400 the sum asked for.

The old houses of the Close help one to conjure up a vision of what the "heart of Exeter" was like before a degenerate age sanctioned the abuses which provoked the ire of Robert Southey as he listened to the bells ringing for the victory of Admiral Mitchell over the Franco-Dutch fleet. "Great Peter" (brought by Bishop Courtenay from Llandaff towards the end of the fifteenth century and recast in 1676) must surely have been silent on that occasion. Upon "Great Peter," said to be the largest bell in England, is rung each evening the curfew. The peal of twelve bells, now in the south tower, is unrivalled both as regards weight and richness of tone. On a calm summer evening their melodious sounds can be heard for many miles echoing over the placid waters of the Exe and the broad estuary far away to the south.

The Chapter House, which the visitor enters from the south transept door, was built by Bishop Bruer, and added to in the episcopacies of Lacy, Nevill, and Bothe (1465–78). When Leofric transferred the Devon See from Crediton to Exeter he gave to the Cathedral the collection of Saxon poetry, which is considered to be a product of the ninth century. The poems comprise the most important book of Anglo-Saxon literature extant. They include Cynewulf's "Christ," "The Legend of St. Juliana," "The Wonders of the Creation," and a metrical life of Guthlac. The collection was printed as the "Codex Exoniensis" in 1842, with translations by Mr. Benjamin Thorpe.

Exeter possesses, in addition to its lovely Cathedral, other interesting ancient churches. In his "Historic Towns" Professor Freeman says : "The city in which Briton and Englishman have had an equal share, the city which has stood so many sieges at the hands of so many enemies—the city which received one William at its eastern gate and the other at its western—the city which still keeps at least the successors of the wall of Athelstan, the minster of Leofric, the castle of Baldwin, and the Guildhall of Shillingford—such a city as this can never lose its historic charm. A typical English city, alike in its greatness and its practical fall from greatness, but more than an English city in its direct connection with two states of things more ancient than the English name in Britain—the city alike of Briton, Roman, and Englishman, the one great prize of the Christian Saxon, the city where Jupiter gave way to Christ, but where Christ never gave way to Woden—British Caerwisc, Roman Isca Damnoniorum, the Anglo-Saxon Exancestre, may well stand first on our roll-call of English Cities. Others can boast of a fuller share of modern greatness ; no other can trace up a life so unbroken to so remote a past."

TRURO CATHEDRAL

THE journey from Exeter to Truro by the Great Western Railway is a delightful one. Objects of interest present themselves to the traveller at every turn, and he seems to have only just crossed the Tamar when he finds himself in the old-world streets of Truro, at once the southernmost, and, in a certain sense at least, one of the youngest, of our English cathedral cities. But if the Cathedral is new the Faith it stands for is old in Cornwall.

In a short history of its ancient Bishopric, the late Bishop Stubbs pointed out that the existence of Roman Christian inscriptions in Cornwall may imply that Christian Truth was within the reach of Cornishmen as early as the fourth century.

The ancient tradition of St. Germans relates the conversion of the people by a Saint of that name sent by Gregory the Great ; but there is no doubt that the St. German in question was the famous Bishop of Auxerre, who lived a century and a half before Pope Gregory, and paid two visits to Britain to confute the Pelagian heresy, the existence of which shows that Christianity, of a sort, was already well established amongst the "West Welsh." The names of the multitudinous Cornish Saints are probably those of the Irish, Welsh, and Breton missionaries. Gildas, the Prince of Damnonia (Cornwall and Devon), became a monk at St. David's in A.D. 589. While there is no historical list of Cornish Bishops, Dr. Stubbs says legend has preserved the names of some ; and there is at Canterbury a letter written by Kenstec or Kenstet, Bishop-elect of the Cornish people, in which he declares his faith to Ceolnoth, Archbishop of Canterbury, 833–70. Conan, the native Cornish Bishop, was a member of Athelstan's Witenagemot from 931, and Cornwall was from that time an English diocese. Where the See was originally fixed is not now known. St. Germans was the See of Burhwold. The church of St. Petrock at Bodmin was a frequent residence of the Cornish Bishops, while Kenstec's See was fixed in the monastery called Dinnurin, possibly Dingerein, the City of King Gerein, now Gerrans or St. Gerrans.

Cornwall, which became an archdeaconry under the Bishops of Exeter, probably in the latter part of the eleventh century, was reconstructed as a diocese with its See at Truro in 1876, with Dr. Edward White Benson, afterwards Archbishop of Canterbury, as the first bishop. Anxious to link the newly formed See with the ancient

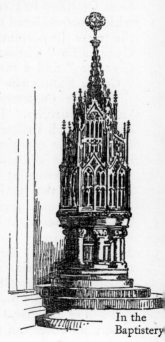

In the
Baptistery

TRURO CATHEDRAL

TRURO CATHEDRAL: THE REREDOS

memories of the early Cornish Church, Dr. Benson attached to each stall of the Honorary Canons the name of some early missionary Bishop or other renowned saint from the old Celtic kalendars.

The foundation-stone of Truro Cathedral, which stands on the site of old St. Mary's Church, was laid on May 20, 1880, by King Edward VII (then Duke of Cornwall), who was also present at the consecration of the Choir, Transepts, Baptistery, and a portion of the Nave on November 3, 1887. The glorious building, complete in every detail, even to spires and turrets, lacking only its Chapter House and Library,* looks down on the former abode of the Boscawens, the Robartses, the Vivians, and many other Cornish families. Built in accordance with the plans of the late Sir J. L. Pearson, R.A., the interior is both dignified and harmonious. The style is Early English, with characteristics of the first part of the thirteenth century. "Students of the architecture of our old English Cathedrals," says a writer, "will now and again be met, as they walk round and through Truro Cathedral, with some feature which reminds them of Lincoln, or Westminster, or some other noble ancient minster; but it will be like the features of children of the same family, born of the same noble parents, Religion and Art, and not mere dead mechanical copies, without life or meaning." It is a sermon in stone worthy to rank with the work of the master-builders of our great historic fanes. Few of the ancient cathedrals can boast of a more beautiful Reredos, or a richer set of eastern windows. The Baptistery, built to commemorate the labours of Henry Martyn, the devoted Indian missionary, who was a native of Truro (1781–1812), is one of the architectural gems of the edifice, with its carved groined roof supported by pillars of Bath and Polyphant stone, and a pavement of local marbles. To John Wesley, who made a great impression on the Cornish miners, there is tribute in a stained-glass window, showing him preaching in the Gwennap Pit. Under this window is now placed the Book of Remembrance, containing the names of 3000 Cornishmen who fell in the Great War.

A good view of the interior can be obtained from under the central tower. Eastward is the lofty, well-proportioned Choir, and a fine Pulpit containing figures of our Lord, Noah, Moses, Elijah, St. John

The Robartes Monument

* The Dean and Chapter possess some valuable books bequeathed to the See of Cornwall by the Rev. Frank Parker and others.

he Baptist, and St. Paul. The Reredos is an elaborate piece of sculpture, depicting the Crucifixion of our Lord, and, above, "The glory which did follow," and on either side are Biblical subjects, with figures of the Apostles, Saints, Martyrs, and Prophets. From the south ambulatory the visitor enters the south aisle of the old Parish Church of St. Mary, with its typical West Country wagon roof, now unfortunately bereft of its panels, and an interesting inlaid eighteenth-century pulpit.

Preserved in this aisle, as in so many of the Cornish churches, is a copy of a letter of thanks written by Charles I to the inhabitants of Cornwall, " given in our camp at Sudley Castle, September 10th, 1643," in which the King says : " That so long as the History of these Times and this nation shall continue, the memory of how much that County (Cornwall) hath merited from us and our Crown may be derived with it to posterity." The visitor should not fail to note the elaborate Tudor carving on the outside of this aisle.

In the Crypt, which contains one or two monuments from the old Parish Church, is a stone to " The pious and well-deserved memory of Owen Fitzpen." Fitzpen, *alias* Phippen, was taken captive by the Turks in March 1627. " He projected sundry plots for his liberty and on yᵉ 17 June 1627 with ten other Christian subjects, Dutch and French, performed by his counsel and courage, he began a cruel fight with 65 Turkes in their own ship, which lasted 3 hours, in which 6 of his Company were slaine, yet God made him captaine, so he brought the ship into Cartagene, being of 400 tons and 22 ordnance. The King sent for him to Madrid to see him, and he was offered a Captain's place and the King's favour if he would turne Papist, which he refused." Fitzpen returned to England and died at Lammorran ten years later. In the southern transept is a memorial brass to Archbishop Benson. The tracery of the rose window was the gift of the masters and boys of Wellington College, of which Dr. Benson was at one time headmaster. The fine central tower, 250 feet high, was the gift of Mr. J. Hawke Dennis, as a memorial to Queen Victoria. The two western towers built by Mrs. Christopher Hawkins as a memorial to her husband, both 204 feet in height, were named in 1910 by royal permission after King Edward VII (S.W.) and Queen Alexandra (N.W.) respectively. There is much to linger over in this Cathedral, which, with the exception of St. Paul's, is the most important and artistic ecclesiastical building erected in England in Post-Reformation times. What will impress the visitor is the splendid devotion of those who by their labours and their offerings rendered possible this latter-day monument to their faith.

GLOUCESTER CATHEDRAL

GLOUCESTER CATHEDRAL: THE NAVE, LOOKING EAST

GLOUCESTER CATHEDRAL: THE ENTRANCE

GLOUCESTER CATHEDRAL: THE CLOISTERS

Facing page 57

GLOUCESTER CATHEDRAL

LOUCESTER CATHEDRAL, formerly the conventual church of the great Benedictine Abbey of St. Peter's, has certain features which are unsurpassed, if not unique. Its majestic square Tower dominates the level valley of the Severn and forms, as it were, a lighthouse for the surrounding neighbourhood. Its South Transept seems to have been the birthplace of the Perpendicular style of architecture (1330), and the Choir, with its considerable height (85 feet), in which the Perpendicular is embroidered over the earlier Norman, is one of the most magnificent conceptions of the Middle Ages. Its East window is a war memorial of local soldiers who fought at Crécy in 1346. The Great Cloister, with its fan-tracery, was built about forty years later. The Lady Chapel, with its beautiful modern glass at the sides and its fifteenth-century East window, was built about 1480. The tomb of Edward II was a great centre of pilgrimage. The Cathedral has for long been the home of sacred music under a series of well-known organists, and here, once in three years, the Three Choirs Musical Festival is held. These meetings take place in rotation at Gloucester, Worcester, and Hereford, and were first instituted in 1724.

The above epitomises the famous Cathedral Church of St. Peter, Gloucester's great and glorious edifice, the lineal successor of a religious house erected on or near its site by Osric, the Christian *sub regulus* of Etheldred, King of Mercia in 681. The Cathedral contains much of the work of Serlo, appointed Abbot of St. Peter's by William the Conqueror in 1072.

This ancient Cathedral and its precincts have seen many incidents in our history. It was in the Chapter House, they say, that the Conqueror decided upon the compilation of the Domesday Book. In the great church in 1093 Anselm was consecrated Archbishop of Canterbury; and there also on October 28, 1216, the boy King, Henry III, was crowned amid great rejoicing and festivity, in the presence of many bishops and nobles, strengthened by the Royal acceptance of the Great Charter which had been wrung from John. In the Great Hall of the Monastery the Parliaments of Henry I, Edward I, Richard II, and Henry IV and V assembled. Just outside the Cathedral Bishop John Hooper, like Ferrar, Bishop of St. David's, suffered martyrdom at the stake for the sake of Protestantism, in the reign of Mary. It was from the Cathedral tower, during the month's siege of the city by the forces of Charles I, who was with his troops, that a patient watch was kept for Cromwell's army of relief. When the citizens were almost at the end of their resources the watch-fires of the Parliamentarians were seen afar off. The longed for relief was at hand. Essex was successful in raising the siege.

Details of the early history of the Saxon Monastery can be gained from the introduction to " Historia et Cartularium Monasterii Sancti Petri Gloucestriæ," by Mr. William Hart, F.S.A. Osric carried out the building under the auspices of Theodore, Archbishop of Canterbury, and Bosel, first Bishop of Worcester. Kyneburga, sister of Osric, who was the first abbess, governed, says an old writer, for twenty-nine years and was buried in the Conventual Church near her brother. For fifty years from the death of Eva, who succeeded her, there was no abbess, but " when Beornwulf became King of Mercia he, seeing so deplorable a state of things, rebuilt the Monastery and changed its formation, placing there secular clergy for the most part married, differing but little from laymen." In A.D. 862 Burgred, King of Mercia, confirmed all the donations which his predecessors had made to the foundation, and freed St. Peter's and all its dependents from all lay services and exactions on condition only " that night and day for ever there should not cease to be offered up prayers for him and his descendants." The secular clergy continued until 1022 (the period of the great monastic revival), when they were supplanted by Benedictine monks at the request of King Cnut, with Edric as the first abbot.

According to Dugdale,* Mr. Hart tells us, the substitution of the new Benedictine rule for that of the secular clergy was " not pleasing to the citizens of Gloucester ; the monks found hatred and persecution at their hands, nay violence was even resorted to, for seven of them were killed by a wealthy nobleman, Wulphin de Rue ; but for an atonement for this crime he was compelled to maintain at his own cost seven monks in the Monastery."

In 1058 Aldred, Bishop of Worcester, built a new church in honour of St. Peter, which thirty years later was burned down. The Monastery seems to have declined in importance, for Serlo, appointed Abbot by the Conqueror, in 1072 on the advice of Osmund, his Chancellor, found there only two monks and eight novices, and was obliged to appeal for assistance to Agelwy, Abbot of Evesham, who had been consecrated at Gloucester. In 1089 Serlo started another church, which was dedicated by the Bishops of Worcester, Rochester, Hereford, and Bangor with " much pomp and magnificence on July 15, 1100." Of Serlo's work William of Malmesbury wrote : " How much the grace of God, conspiring with his industry, elevated the place, what eloquence can explain ? The management of the Abbey in spirituals is what the weak may look up to, the strong not despise. This was effected by the discipline of Serlo, a man humble to the good, but menacing and terrible to the proud." It is to Serlo that the foundations of the present Cathedral are due.

Throughout the thirteenth century there was apparently great building activity at the Monastery, but some of this work has disappeared. Abbot Thokey, who in 1318 built at great expense the south aisle of the Nave, was in office at the time of the assassination of Edward II at Berkeley Castle. It is recorded that as soon as the news of the murder became known at St. Peter's, Thokey, " with his convent, accompanied with a procession of the whole city, went to Berkeley and brought away in his chariot the corpse of the unfortunate King. After his body had been viewed by several persons appointed for the

---

* " Memoriale Ecclesiæ Gloucestriæ Compendiarium."

GLOUCESTER

HEREFORD

WORCESTER

purpose, the King was decently and privately buried by the Abbey to which he had been a great benefactor." Edward III, in consideration of the great expense which had been incurred by the Abbey for his father's funeral, conferred substantial privileges upon St. Peter's, and granted it, in perpetuity, the Hundred of Dudstone, with all its emoluments and appurtenances, at the fee farm rent of £12 per annum. To the memory of Edward II Edward III erected the beautiful canopied shrine on the north side of the Choir, the finest monument in the Cathedral. " Edward's shrine," says an old writer, " was so frequented by people that the city was scarce sufficient to contain them, and their offerings were so great that it was thought they would have been enough to have built the whole church."

Walter Froucester, the historian of the Abbey, and its first mitred abbot, built the Great Cloister ; while Abbot Seabrooke, who died in 1457, began the beautiful Central Tower, committing the continuance of the work to the care of Robert Tully, a monk who was clerk of the works if not the actual architect who later became Bishop of St. David's. In the Choir, over the arch of the tower, is the following :

HOC QUOD DIGESTUM SPECULARIS OPUSQUE POLITUM
TULLI HAEC EX ONERE, SEBROKE ABBATE JUBENTE.

This couplet has been anglicised thus :

" *This fabric which you see exact and neat*
The Abbot charged the monk to see compleat."

The finely proportioned tower rises to a height of 225 feet, with four pinnacles of singularly delicate grace. Abbots Henley and Farley (1457–98) were responsible for the Lady Chapel, which has been admirably described as " a complete specimen of richness and chastity of composition, most aptly suited with a fine eastern window. The roof is one grand pointed arch indented on the sides by the arches of the window." The chapel is much narrower at its western end than at the eastern which enables the light effectively to reach the great East window of the Choir. In size, the Lady Chapel ranks next to Henry VII's chapel at Westminster Abbey. Near the altar are two beautiful transepts, above each of which are minstrels' galleries. The hangings at the back of the altar hide the mutilated reredos, the work of Cromwellian soldiery.

The lofty and graceful Choir, probably unequalled in England, is particularly noticeable for the richness of its vaulting—carried out by Adam de Staunton (1337–51)—and the elaborate Perpendicular tracery over Norman work. On either side is an apsidal chapel. The Great East Window enhances the beauty of the Choir. The east end of the original Norman Choir was semi-circular. To insert the great window, the two easternmost bays were removed and the walls were sloped outwards, so that the window extends beyond the normal width of the Choir. The window is the largest in England, being

59

162 square feet in excess of that at York Minster with an area of 2,736 square feet. As already stated it is a memorial to men who fell at Crécy. The canopied Choir stalls are the work of Abbot de Staunton and Abbot Horton. Opposite the Episcopal throne is a special chair for the mayor of Gloucester. The misericords will attract attention because of the grotesque ornamentation —two knights are represented playing dice, a knight is running at the tilt, another is beheading a giant, a forester is shown killing a stag, another shows the shepherds following the Star of Bethlehem, while another tells the story of King Alexander's flight by means of two birds chained to a basket in which the monarch is seated. Above the Choir, extending from one side to the other and built in octagonal form, is the Abbot's Gallery. This, owing to its peculiar acoustic properties, has been termed the Whispering Gallery. At the eastern end of the Gallery are the remains of an altar of unhewn stone, on each side of which, we are told, the Abbot and others were accustomed to stand to hear Divine Service performed in the Lady Chapel.

The Great Cloister on the north of the Nave is the most perfect of its kind in this country. It is sublimely beautiful. The visitor is unconsciously forced by this great master-work to linger here. The lovely fan-tracery is unrivalled and in a splendid state of preservation. To quote from a description of the Cathedral in the early part of last century, "It is perhaps a fanciful idea of Bishop Warburton that Gothic architecture was intended to imitate an avenue of lofty trees ; yet if the proper colouring were laid on, the same idea would probably strike more ordinary observers on walking through the cloister." At the western end of the north cloister is a long stone trough used as a washing place by the monks. To the south are twenty carrels, or stalls, made for the monks to study and write in. The modern pilgrim, accustomed to high standards of mechanical printing, yet acquainted with the beautiful missals, penmanship, and decorative scrolls of the ancient monasteries, can picture the scene in Froucester's famous cloister when the Benedictine brethren of St. Peter's occupied these carrels. The mind can then be turned to another picture in the history of the cloisters, that when Cromwell—who, it is said, was provoked by the old adage "As sure as God's in Gloucester" to declare that the city had "more churches than godliness"—converted the cloisters into stables for his soldiery. The Chapter House, entered from the cloisters, is a fine Norman structure (1088–1095).

The massive Nave with its impressive Norman characteristics is striking. Separating the nave from the aisles are twelve large circular pillars of unusual height with curious ornamentation. The two westernmost pillars are in the Perpendicular style (circa 1425). Over the Norman pillars on the north side are representations of a tiger's head, a nun, two women, a man with long hair, and a tonsured monk, and over the south side a monk, a youth, a head with a cadaverous countenance, a nun, two anchorites, and a hideous mask. The heads serve as brackets to sixteen clusters of short pillars, the capitals of which are richly sculptured with foliage. These support a crude embroidery, on which rest the bases of five other pillars " clustered with capitals of transcendent beauty." Mr. Cresy, in a paper before the Archæological Association at Gloucester in 1846, contended that " the crypt under the Choir, the cylindrical pillars and the walls of the Nave and Choir, the walls of the south transept, and in fact the entire shell of the building, was Saxon structure, though altered materially by the Normans and their successors." The Crypt, which forms one great underground church beneath the choir and the aisles, other authorities state, is purely Norman work, and ranks among the four apsidal crypts in this country, the others being at Canterbury, Winchester, and Worcester.

Besides the shrine of Edward II there are many ancient monuments and tombs of great interest. On the north side of the High Altar near the entrance to the Lady Chapel is the tomb of Osric (Osricus rex primus fundator hujus monasterii). In the south aisle Humphry Bohun, Earl of Hereford, is buried. Other tombs worthy of inspection are those of Robert Curthose, Duke of Normandy, the eldest son of William the Conqueror, who gave considerable benefactions to the Monastery, Abbot Foliot, a successor of Serlo, who was conspicuous in the controversy between Henry II and Thomas Becket, Abbot Seabroke, the builder of the Cathedral tower, Bishop Warburton, Edward Jenner, to whom we owe the discovery of the use of vaccine in combating small pox, and that of John Gower, who finished the Gothic work of the church, depicting the master mason with his tools, and his son showing the different orders of Gothic, in the Choir.

In " Great Peter " Gloucester possesses one of the largest bells in England, and nothing can exceed the beauty of the Cathedral chimes, each composed by a musician of repute.

While at Gloucester the visitor will no doubt visit the ancient churches in the city. St. Mary de Crypt, which derives its name from the fact that there are two crypts beneath it, dates from 1138. Here George Whitefield, the preacher to whom the religious revival of the eighteenth-century owed so much, was baptised and delivered his first sermon. He died at Newbury port, Mass., on Sept. 30, 1770, The tombs include that of Robert Raikes, the founder of the Sunday School movement. St. Mary-de-Lode contains a monument to John Hooper, who, as before stated, was burned as a heretic in front of Gloucester Cathedral on Feb. 9, 1555 ; St. Nicholas has sixteenth century brasses ; and St. John the Baptist was rebuilt in 1734.

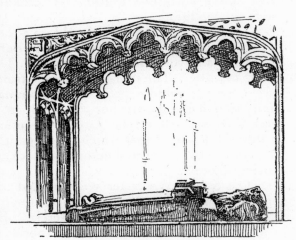

The Tomb of King Osric

WORCESTER CATHEDRAL

CATHEDRALS should never be compared with one another. Each should be enjoyed for its own beauty and associations; and each should be studied for its own special contributions to history and to art. Worcester Cathedral is rich in all these respects.

The exterior of the Cathedral, though massive and finely proportioned, appears disappointingly modern; and the reason is that in the last century, between the years 1857 and 1877, the exterior was very largely refaced. The soft sandstone had perished almost everywhere; and the walls had been disfigured in the preceding two centuries by haphazard repairs. It was often compared to " Joseph's coat of many colours." The refacing of the exterior, and the necessary replacement of perished stone here and there in the interior, were carried out with singular modesty and self-suppression by the architect, Mr. Perkins. It was done so admirably that Professor Willis, whose prolonged study of the Cathedral during that period is, from an architectural point of view, of the highest value, could say that " we now have a reproduction of the original aspect of the Cathedral, so far as that can be determined." No praise could be higher or better deserved. On Mr. Perkin's death, which happened shortly before the restoration of the interior was finished, the Chapter appointed in his place Sir Gilbert Scott, to whom are due the screens and other features in the Choir which to present taste and judgment appear somewhat incongruous. Part of the interior—the South wall of the north-east transept—is retained, for historical reasons, in its un-restored condition.

The visitor on entering should go at once to the west end of the Cathedral. There his first impression of the interior will be that of unity and harmony in design and colouring of the whole. The Cathedral is beheld as a whole in all its dignity. The roof-ridge is seen from end to end, the view is not blocked by screen or reredos. A close examination, however, will show that the unity and harmony are not the result of uniformity of style, as at Salisbury and Cologne, but of the natural evolution, through four centuries, of each historic style out of that which preceded it.

And here it will not be out of place to give a little of the history of this ancient diocese.

The See of Worcester was founded in 679 by Archbishop Theodore, as one of the five into which he divided the huge diocese of Lichfield, embracing the whole central kingdom of Mercia. He sent to Worcester Bishop Bosel, a pupil of the learned Hilda, Abbess of Whitby. The Worcestershire diocese, which included also Warwickshire and Gloucestershire, was then fiercely heathen. Three hundred years later, after churches and schools and monasteries had been founded far and wide as centres of light, Worcester

WORCESTER CATHEDRAL

WORCESTER CATHEDRAL: THE CHOIR

Facing page 63

itself, which had been a great missionary centre, became monastic, under the influence of its two bishops, Dunstan and Oswald, and of King Edgar. The College of Clergy at Worcester became a great Benedictine monastery.

To this monastery, early in the eleventh century, the young Saxon Wulstan came as a monk, and rose in succession to be schoolmaster, precentor, prior, and finally bishop ; and when in 1066 William the Norman became by conquest King of England, Wulstan was one of the Bishops who crowned him, and was the only Saxon Bishop who was not ejected from his See.

In 1084 Bishop Wulstan, now an old man, made the design of this Cathedral, on the magnificent scale of the Norman churches ; and before his death in 1095 he saw the Crypt completed, and probably the Presbytery over it, and part at least of the Tower, Main Transepts, and Nave. His untouched work is still to be seen in the Crypt—unique and quite the most beautiful crypt in the world—and in two shafts and capitals, one at the north-east corner of the north Nave aisle, the other at the north-west corner of the south Choir aisle. These survive, and show the Norman style in its early and perfect simplicity.

The next stage in the evolution of church architecture is to be seen in the Chapter House, built in the Decorated Norman style of the early twelfth century. This Chapter House is also unique, in its circular form, and in its artistic use of the green Highley sandstone and the white Cotswold limestone ; and is remarkable also for the first appearance of a central shaft and radiating ribs. The exterior casing of the Chapter House in red stone, its decagonal form, its buttresses, and its windows, are due to a partial repair made in the fifteenth century. Some traces of the same Decorated Norman style will be noted in the Nave, two bays distant from the west end, and show that part of the Nave was built at about the same date.

The next, and an even greater, step in evolution is shown in the two western bays of the Nave, built about 1170. The great square piers of the Crypt are now modified, and they are enriched by pilasters and shafts attached. The barrel arches of the Crypt are transformed and divided into members, the capitals are carved in white stone, while the ribs are more richly moulded. These two bays, and especially those of the adjacent south aisle, are the most perfect specimen of Transitional Norman of the latter part of the twelfth century existing in England.

The fall of the tower in 1175, and a very destructive fire in 1202, necessitated an extensive repair, or rebuilding, and a re-roofing of the Choir and central part of the Cathedral. Happily large funds poured in, as a result of the canonisation of Wulstan by the Pope in 1203, consequent on the numerous miracles of healing reported and confirmed as taking place at his tomb in the Choir. On June 7, 1218, there was a great re-dedication of the Cathedral, now restored and adorned in the most perfect style then attained, known as " Early English." To this dedication the young King Henry III came, and an unprecedented number of nobles and bishops were present. The whole of the Choir, and Ladye Chapel, and the eastern transepts are in this style, and are the work of the first half of the thirteenth century. The work may be compared with that at Lincoln, Beverley and Salisbury.

The next stage is seen in the Nave. Early in the fourteenth century rebuilding began at the east end of the north side, in a style developed out of the Early English of the Choir. The seven eastern bays of the north side had been nearly completed when work was interrupted in 1349 by the Black Death. The style of that portion is Decorated. When, after a quarter of a century, work could be resumed, fresh improvements suggested themselves, and the south side of the Nave, the North Porch, and the Tower and Cloisters were rebuilt in the Perpendicular style. The great builder of that period was Bishop Wakefield.

The latest style of architecture shown in the Cathedral is that of Prince Arthur's Chantry, built in 1504 by Henry VII, to contain the remains of his elder son Arthur, who died in early youth at Ludlow. The chantry is highly noteworthy for its carved figures of saints, and for its heraldry.

This is a brief outline of the story of the Cathedral. Visitors to Worcester will find that the whole of the Cathedral is open to them, without any fee, for devotion and study, and that every assistance for these purposes has been provided them. On entrance they will be able to purchase, for three pence, an illustrated handbook written by a member of the Chapter, which will both help them to find at once the points of chief interest, and will serve as a souvenir of their visit. Most of the monuments in the Cathedral are also provided with historical notices, written by the present Dean—the Very Rev. W. Moore Ede, and these notices are also purchaseable as a volume.

For visiting the Crypt and the Chapter House with its varied treasures on view in its show-cases, also for ascending the belfry and tower, with its commanding view of the whole scene of the Battle of Worcester, the attendance of a verger is necessary ; and a small payment is made in support of the Fabric Fund. No gratuities to vergers, however, are allowed.

It must not be forgotten that these great Cathedrals owe their growth and beauty and maintenance largely to the piety of pilgrims in centuries long past, and that it is on the piety and liberality of the visitors and pilgrims of to-day that the Dean and Chapter rely for the means of providing for the constant repairs and attention which such a building needs. Visitors are, therefore, requested not to leave the Cathedral without offering a prayer to God for His blessing, and a suitable gift placed in one of the boxes for the care and upkeep of the Cathedral.

The Refectory, with its fine Majestas, has been used as the King's School since the Reformation, and is, therefore, not open to visitors.

The Library, rich in old books and MSS. and charters and account rolls, is in the south triforium of the Nave, but is not open to visitors in general.

The Cathedral suffered much at the Reformation. The beautiful and jewelled shrines of St. Oswald and St. Wulstan were pillaged and destroyed, and relics burned and scattered as dust. Out of thirty-three altars all but one

WORCESTER CATHEDRAL: THE CLOISTERS

WORCESTER CATHEDRAL: THE CRYPT

Facing page 65

were destroyed. All the Service books were ordered to be collected and burnt. One only escaped, probably by an accident—the Worcester Antiphonar— a unique collection of the music of Benedictine services from the early thirteenth century down to the Reformation. It has now been published in facsimile by the Benedictines of Solesme. Those who wish to study the history and architecture of the Cathedral in detail should refer to the best guide-books, and in particular to the Transactions of the Worcestershire Historical and Archæological Societies.

The Cathedral suffered much also during the Commonwealth. The roofs of a large part of it were stripped of every ounce of lead and of timber ; all its windows were broken up, and the fittings, books, and ornaments plundered or destroyed. A great restoration took place from 1660 to 1666. Partial repairs were subsequently effected from time to time ; but, as above related, another restoration became necessary, and was carried out between 1857 and 1877.

Visitors will see for themselves what care is at the present day taken of this precious monument of English piety, and will see evidence also that it is a living force in the Church of Christ in its City and Diocese.

Worcester, like the adjoining dioceses of Hereford and Gloucester—with which it is associated in the Three Choirs Festival—is noted for the excellence of its music. On Easter Day, 1925, the fine organ which had been reconstructed at a cost of £6,250, and is now a splendid instrument worth £25,000, was re-opened in the presence of the Mayor and Corporation and a large congregation of subscribers to the Restoration Fund.

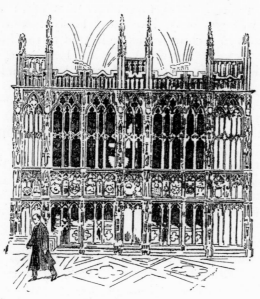

Prince Arthur's Chantry

HEREFORD CATHEDRAL

"T seems probable that the See of Hereford," wrote the Hon. and Very Rev. James W. Leigh, Dean of Hereford, some years ago, " is one of the few bishoprics which have come down almost without interruption from the first establishment of Christianity in our land until the present day. Heylin considered it the most ancient in England; Archbishop Ussher says it was the seat of an Episcopal See in the sixth century, and that one of the bishops attended a Synod convened by the Archbishop of Caerleon A.D. 544, and that a Bishop of Hereford was present at the conference held by St. Augustine in 601." Dean Leigh's statement is confirmed by other authorities, although the first Bishop actually named by most historians is Putta, who was translated to Hereford from the See of Rochester in Kent in 676, three years after it had been decided by a Synod held by Archbishop Theodore that the Mercian dominion should be split up into several new dioceses. When Putta entered his new office the area of the Diocese of Hereford was lessened, and Worcester became the head of a separate See. From the time of Putta—who, the Venerable Bede tells us, was more careful about ecclesiastical than secular matters—there has been an unbroken succession of Prelates at the picturesque Wye city.

Of the Cathedral Church and of the earliest Hereford Bishops there is little accurate information. The first church, thought to have been built prior to A.D. 600, was probably, like most Early Saxon edifices, of wattles or of wood. In A.D. 676 a church was dedicated to the Blessed Virgin Mary. The murder, A.D. 793, at Sutton Walls of Ethelbert, King of the East Anglians, instigated by Offa, King of Mercia, had an important bearing on the future of the Cathedral. Ethelbert's assassination is said to have been due to his wish to marry Ælfrida, Offa's daughter. Her mother, Queen Quendrida, opposed the union, believing, it is said, that, in aspiring to become her son-in-law, Ethelbert was planning to succeed Offa. Ethelbert was buried at Marden " amid supernatural manifestations," and tradition says that the stories of these, added to remorse, led Offa to remove the body to Hereford Cathedral, where it was reinterred beneath an elaborate shrine. It is further recorded that Wilfrid, a viceroy of Egbert, King of Mercia, built a noble church of stone about A.D. 825, and dedicated it to St. Mary and St. Ethelbert.

Bishop Athelstan (*vir magnæ sanctitatis*, according to Florence of Worcester), who found the church in a great state of decay (A.D. 1012), practically rebuilt it. Athelstan, although blind for thirteen years before his death in A.D. 1056, directed the affairs of the See with great fervour, and it must have been a heavy blow to him when his Cathedral was burned down

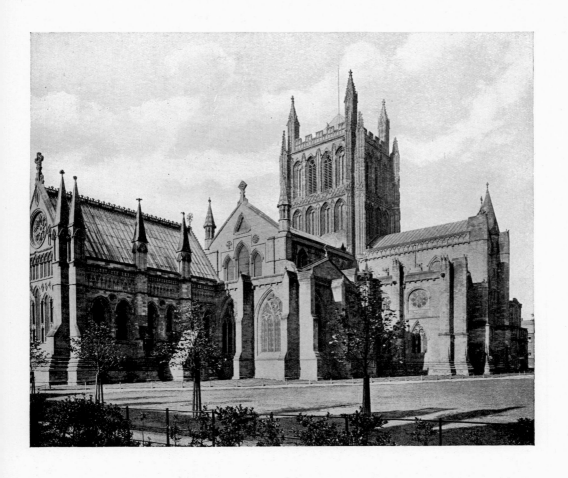

HEREFORD CATHEDRAL

HEREFORD CATHEDRAL: THE NAVE AND NORTH ARCADE

in A.D. 1055 by a Welsh horde which overran the city. "They burned the town and the great mynstre, which the venerable Bishop Athelstan had before caused to be built, that they plundered and bereaved of relics and of vestments and of all things and slew the folk and led some away." *

Twenty years elapsed before any attempt was made to raise another Cathedral. The task fell to the lot of Robert Losinga of Lorraine, the first Norman Bishop, who is thought to have taken as his pattern the basilica of Aix-la-Chapelle. Losinga erected the Choir, Transepts, and Choir aisles, his original plan being carried on by Bishop Reynelm—whose monument in the Choir contains the phrase " Fundator Ecclesiæ "—and completed in 1148 by Bishop R. de Betun. About A.D. 1180–90 the Gothic or Pointed style began to be developed at Hereford as elsewhere, and the eastern apses of the Norman church gave way to Transitional work, a considerable portion of which still remains to be seen at the Ambulatory or crossing of the Eastern Transept west of the Lady Chapel. The North Transept was transformed by pointed arches and windows of a very original kind under the direction of Bishop Peter de Aquablanca (1240–68).

It scarcely needs apology to digress from the progress of the Cathedral to the stage at which we now see it, in order to take up again the immensely interesting history of the See. The archives of the Dean and Chapter are singularly informative, and a great debt of gratitude is owing to Canon W. W. Capes for his translation of the charters and records of the Cathedral. Canon Capes marshalled a long series of charters containing grants from the Norman and Angevin monarchs, who are sometimes spoken of as the founders and benefactors of the Church at Hereford. "Documentary evidence," says Canon Capes, " implies that the liberality chiefly came from the rulers and nobles of Saxon England. The Conqueror indeed restored manors to the See of which it had been deprived by Harold, but his successors were mostly content to issue licences for fairs and markets on episcopal domains, or to confirm possessions enjoyed before, or to sanction forest rights. The grant of sixty acres near Hereford made by Richard I is the chief exception to the rule."

Men of all classes were moved by the glorious ideals and the Faith of which Hereford Cathedral is a symbol. The rich and noble, Canon Capes shows, were not the only benefactors, for there are many charters in which the offerings of tradesmen and mechanics are recorded. One deals with the rent-charge of 1d. by Richard de Medimor on land in Madeley ; John, the cook's son (*Johannes Filius Radulphi coci*), gives a ground rent of 2d. " to the church of Hereford " ; Dean Jordan gave land in A.D. 1175 " to brew good beer for the canons." David d'Aqua, after purchasing land to increase the income of his prebend, gave tithe of it about the same time to provide money for a distribution among the clergy of simnel cakes, which were eaten in his memory from that day forward till the ministers of Queen Elizabeth had the little fund diverted for an usher in the Cathedral School ; another kindly

---

* Anglo-Saxon Chronicle.

spirit, Elyas of Bristol, bethought him, in A.D. 1230, of "ampler commons of bread and beer."

In the thirteenth and part of the fourteenth centuries the Cathedral lacked funds. During Bishop Hugh Ffoliot's period of office the hospital of St. Ethelbert in Hereford was founded, the citizens pledging themselves to pay for its support "a tithe of their fair on St. Denis Day; and the Abbot and convent of Bristol showed their sympathy by substantial offerings of beans."

Ffoliot it was who excommunicated the citizens for unjustly distraining on his tenants for the payment of local rates. Peter de Aquablanca, a Southern Frenchman, we read in Canon Capes' work, stamped his influence most markedly on the dignities and fabric of the Cathedral and "carried through with little scruple financial expedients which were in the interest of the English Crown and the Papal Court, and which made him perhaps the most detested man throughout the religious houses and rectories of England, causing Matthew of Paris to write of him that his memory 'exhaled a sulphurous stench.'" His agent Bernard, Prior of Champagne, was much detested, and was murdered in the Chapel of St. Mary Magdalene—*non religiosus sed irreligiosus* (Ann. Tewksb.).

Peter de Aquablanca rebuilt the North Transept, which can be compared

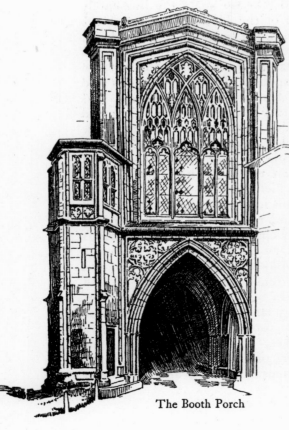

with the earlier Norman work, and "discontented canons who disliked the innovations were forced by papal bull to bear their share of the expenses." Peter unsuccessfully appealed in 1250 to Henry III and to Rome to sweep away ancient precedents in matters concerning the rights of the Dean and Chapter. He, however, was too generous to harbour long any ill-feeling for those who had opposed him, and vested in the Dean and Chapter the control of the charity he had endowed with lands at Holme Lacy, and made other benefactions. Bishop Peter, Dean Leigh tells us, is said to have been the prelate "whom Robin Hood robbed in the glades of merry Barnsdale."

Of the many interesting Herefordian documents the reader is tempted to linger longest over those relating to St. Thomas de Cantilupe, the Bishop of Hereford who was canonised in A.D. 1320. Cantilupe was the son of William, Lord Cantilupe and his wife Millicent, Countess of Evreux. He died near Orvieto. While his bones were being conveyed into Hereford Cathedral, says an old writer, "Gilbert, Earl of Gloucester, approached and touched the casket which

The Booth Porch

68

HEREFORD CATHEDRAL: TOMB OF THOMAS OF HEREFORD

HEREFORD CATHEDRAL: TWELFTH CENTURY FONT

contained them ' whereupon they bled afresh.' " So deeply impressed was the Earl that he made "full restitution of all lands which Bishop Cantilupe had rightly claimed of him." Marvels of faith-healing associated with the name of Cantilupe (Canon Capes writes) and the recognition of his sanctity brought many pilgrims to his shrine. A fabric roll shows that over £4000 of our money was given in one year by devotees " attracted by the fame of the wonder worker," which sum enabled the erection and the decoration of the central tower to be undertaken ; insecure foundations were underpinned, the aisles rebuilt and much of the Eastern Transept was reconstructed.

In 1359, Canon Capes tells us, the Chapter contracted with an Evesham builder to devote the remainder of his working life to the Cathedral for 3s. a week and a daily loaf of bread, and to give instructions in the arts of masonry and carpentering to the labourers under him.

From the thirteenth century the changes and additions to the Cathedral may be arranged chronologically as follows :

THIRTEENTH CENTURY OR EARLY ENGLISH : The Ladye Chapel and Crypt, the Clerestory of the Choir, and the north transept, a remarkable piece of work, *circa* 1260.

FOURTEENTH CENTURY OR DECORATED : The rebuilding of the Choir and Nave aisles, the inner north porch, the north and south ends of the eastern transept, the central tower, a western tower, now destroyed, and the Chapter House, now unfortunately in ruins.

FIFTEENTH CENTURY OR PERPENDICULAR : The first of this period here began about 1400 by alterations in the south transept, followed by the Stanbury Chantry Chapel 1470, and the Audley Chapel 1500 ; the Cloisters also belong to this period, and finally the North or Booth porch, completing the pre-Reformation church.

Norman Arches

In 1786 the western tower, originally built it is believed by De Braose, fell, carrying with it two bays of the Nave, one of which has never been rebuilt. The present triforium and clerestory of the Nave are the work of James Wyatt, 1786–96, replacing the magnificent Norman work which he wantonly destroyed.

The West Front, reconstructed by Wyatt after the collapse of the tower, has now been replaced by work designed by Mr. John Oldrid Scott, 1901–7, which has added considerably to the beauty of the building. It presents a handsome façade containing sculptured figures, and includes a stained glass window to the memory of Queen Victoria, the gift of the women of Herefordshire.

The massive central tower (1320–40), the decorated work of which is enriched with ball-flower ornament, was at one time surmounted by a timber spire. The North or Booth porch, noticeable for its fine windows, the arcading on the Ladye Chapel, and the north transept are other ſtriking features of the exterior.

Although from the point of view of size Hereford is one of the smaller Cathedrals, it is an architeċtural gem, for, in the opinion of the late Sir Gilbert Scott, few English Cathedrals have a more perfeċt series of specimens of the different ſtyles of English architeċture. The visitor can see here examples of all the fashions of architeċture in use in this country during the five centuries preceding the sixteenth. The outside length of the Cathedral is 342 feet; inside, 327 feet 5 inches; Nave, 158 feet 6 inches; Choir from screen to reredos, 75 feet 6 inches; Ladye Chapel, 93 feet 5 inches.

Hereford, like the neighbouring Cathedrals of Worceſter and Glouceſter which share the Triennial Choir Feſtival, has been noted for the excellence of its music. It was Bishop Putta who foſtered the teaching of the Gregorian Tones introduced by St. Auguſtine to England, and to the use of which Archbishop Theodore gave his support. From A.D. 1215 Hereford possessed its own liturgy, known as " The Hereford Use," and in that conneċtion is one of the cities referred to in the Book of Common Prayer preface, the others being York, Salisbury, Lincoln, and Bangor. A fine thirteenth-century MS. of the Hereford Use, containing a quantity of choicely illuminated church music, is one of the Cathedral's moſt cherished treasures.

In a chamber over the weſt Cloiſter is the Library, noteworthy for its chained books, which were for 200 years kept in the Ladye Chapel, almoſt unseen and unknown until the reſtoration of the chapel by Cottingham. There are over 2000 chained volumes, the largest colleċtion of such works in England, a number of much-valued manuscripts, and twenty-four editions of the Bible in various tongues, some dating back to A.D. 1567–1611. Here are preserved a manuscript copy of the Gospels bequeathed by Athelſtan in A.D. 1055, dating from the ninth century and illuminated in Celtic ſtyle ; a copy of " The Golden Legend," printed by Caxton (A.D. 1483) ; the Nuremberg Chronicle (A.D. 1493) with woodcuts by Albert Dürer ; and several examples of early Venetian printing.

In a case on the eaſt wall of the South Transept is the celebrated " Mappa Mundi." " The map is probably, to a great extent," says Mr. J. W. Jeudwine, in a chapter on Mediæval Maps in his entertaining book, " The Firſt Twelve Centuries of British Story," " copied from one by Henry of Mainz, which was inserted in a description of the world dedicated to Matilda, the mother of Henry II. With a prophetic eye the map-maker draws the British Isles out of all proportion to the reſt of Europe." The map, probably executed by a Canon of Hereford about 1300, is of interest as showing the change in foreign relations which had come over the islands since the accession of Henry II. " In Norway the monkey is shown, possibly denoting the commercial conneċtion with the Eaſt." The north in this map is in some respeċts, Mr. Jeudwine considers, almoſt as elementary as those on the maps executed by the Spanish monk Beatus. The North Sea has been

HEREFORD CATHEDRAL: THE CHAINED LIBRARY

HEREFORD CATHEDRAL: "NUREMBERG CHRONICLE"; *centre*, CAXTON'S
"GOLDEN LEGEND"; "HEREFORD USE" *and* "ANGLO-SAXON CHRONICLE"

entirely squeezed out. The Faroes, Iceland, and the Shetlands lie in line west of Norway, and the Orkneys are represented by a large circular island surrounded by smaller ones, a description more applicable to the Shetlands. The map contains the names of a number of cities in Great Britain which had by this time assumed some importance in political life. Referring to the amount of detail given for the south of Europe as compared with " the monstrosities and fabulous details " of the east and north, Mr. Jeudwine points out that all the maps of this period were pictures of nations on the shores of the Mediterranean Sea, drawn by men whose interests were solely in Rome and the East. " One ought not to be too critical of the wild romance which furnished illustrations for this work of art, the Biblical stories, the heathen mythologies, the mediæval legends, which appear in this map more freely than in many others much earlier. The men of that day had suddenly been brought face to face with the greatest of all miracles, the illumination of the Biblical story, the epitome of the heathen mythology, the source of the mediæval legend. . . . No miracle, no phantasm, no creation of abnormal life seemed impossible to the men of that day."

Another much-prized treasure is a chasse or reliquary, resembling the Limoges work of the early thirteenth century, consisting of a casket with figures, pronounced by experts to be a picture of the Martyrdom of Thomas Becket.

The latter-day pilgrim will enjoy the Cloisters, and the grandeur of the Bishop's Palace and other buildings which breathe the spirit which has permeated the Cathedral City of Hereford throughout the centuries.

Since the description of Hereford Cathedral contained in the preceding pages was printed, the Crypt has been restored by the benefaction of Sir Henry Webb, in memory of his son, Basil, who fell in the Great War. The Crypt which, like the Ladye Chapel above it, is a beautiful specimen of Early English architecture, built soon after 1200 A.D., has for many generations been desolate from disuse ; and it is a cause for great satisfaction that it has once more been opened as a place of worship. The areas outside the windows have been thrown back so as to admit more light to the chapel ; the walls have been carefully brushed, but not scraped ; a clean, bright floor of stone has been laid ; and the little sanctuary has been furnished with an altar of stone surmounted by a reredos in which are figures of St. Michael, St. George, and St. Ethelbert, the work of Sir William Goscombe John, R.A.

Another graceful addition to the beauties of the Cathedral is that of eight small windows which have been placed in the Stanbury Chapel, as a gift of Mr. Lennox Lee, of How Caple Court. Mr. Lee, who is an old Etonian, wished to commemorate in Stanbury's chantry the bishop's association with his old school. A reference to the archives of Eton College has shown that Bishop Stanbury was not, as has sometimes been stated, its first Provost ; but, as confessor to King Henry VI, he seems to have been much consulted by his sovereign over the plans of the royal foundation, and, perhaps, he might have been its first Provost if he had been willing to accept the office. The stained glass, in two series of four windows each, is the work of the Bromsgrove Guild, and represents the foundation of Eton College and the enthronement of Stanbury as Bishop of Hereford.

Before long there will be placed in the Cathedral a memorial bust of John Percival, Bishop of Hereford from 1895 to 1918, the work of Mr. Allan Wyon, and some fine fragments of fourteenth and fifteenth century glass which were removed from the Cathedral, as is believed, after the fall of the Western Tower in 1786, and, after being for more than a century in Hampton Court, Herefordshire, have been returned to the Cathedral by the generosity of Mr. R. Grosvenor Thomas and Mr. Wilfrid Drake.

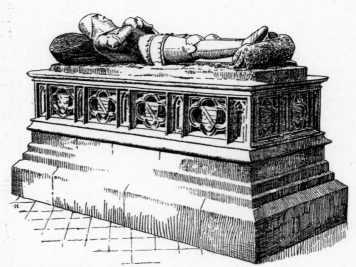

Tomb of Sir Richard Pembridge, one of the first three Garter Knights

72

CHRIST CHURCH (OXFORD): THE NAVE

CHRIST CHURCH (OXFORD): SHRINE OF ST. FRIDESWIDE

OXFORD CATHEDRAL

"TO most Oxford men—indeed to the common visitor of Oxford—the town seems a mere offshoot of the University. Its appearance is largely modern ; it presents hardly any monument that can vie in antiquity with the venerable fronts of the colleges and halls. An isolated church here and there tells a different tale ; but the largest of its parish churches is best known as the church of the University, and the church of St. Frideswide, which might suggest even to a careless observer some idea of the town's greatness before university life began, is known to visitors simply as Christ Church Chapel."

Christ Church Chapel, to which the late J. R. Green alludes in the foregoing extract from his " Oxford Studies," is the splendid Cathedral Church of Christ, which has served the needs of the diocese of Oxford besides performing the functions of a college chapel since 1546. It is a beautiful Norman edifice containing many signs of the liberality bestowed upon it later by Wolsey in the days when he wished to show his regard for his Alma Mater by founding the Cardinal College. The Cathedral, once the church of the Priory of St. Frideswide, possesses an antiquity far greater than the venerable college with which it is associated.

The story of Frideswide (her name is translated as the " Bond of Peace ") is pictured in a stained glass window in the Latin Chapel by Burne-Jones, one of Oxford's distinguished *alumni*. In cold prose we are told that on the site of Christ Church a convent was founded in 727 by Didan, Subregulus, or Earl, of Oxford, who dedicated it to the Holy Trinity. Didan's only daughter Frideswide, who had prevailed upon her father to found the convent, became its head. According to old writers she was " brought up in all manner of honest and liberal breeding befitting her descent," and was much sought after in marriage : " Algar, Earl of Leicester, had been inflamed with the lure of this lady, and coveted her, though sacred and forbidden, for his wife. On her concealing herself from him in a wood at Bampton, twelve miles from Oxford, the city was threatened with destruction by fire unless she were found. Such tyranny and presumption could not escape Divine vengeance : he was struck blind ! Hence arose such a dread of the Kings of Britain that none of his successors dared enter Oxford for some time after."

Frideswide died in 735. The Priory became the property of secular canons. In 1002, when St. Frideswide was a parish church, there took place on St. Brice's Day the massacre of the Danes by order of King Æthelred the Unrede. Some Danes having taken refuge in the tower of the church, it was set on fire to ensure their destruction. Two years later Æthelred repented of his act and started rebuilding the church, assisted, it is believed, by his brother-in-law, Robert Duke of Normandy. The fine capitals in the choir are believed by some to be the work of this period.

That a church was raised is confirmed by the Domesday Book, which shows that secular canons were there in 1086. Soon after this date these were replaced by Augustinian canons. To this church Henry I and Malcolm, King of Scotland, made benefactions, but fire also devastated it. In 1120 Prior Guimond (1111–1150), who was Henry's Chaplain, undertook work of restoration and was responsible for the Norman doorway of the Chapter House. By a charter of Henry I in 1122 the monastery was formally founded. Under the guidance of Prior Robert of Cricklade the main fabric of the present cathedral was commenced in 1160. Prior Robert also founded a school which is " considered the original germ of the University." Twenty years later the remains of St. Frideswide were removed " from an obscure to a more noted place in the church." This first translation of the Saint's bones was arranged by Prior Philip, and carried out in the presence of the Archbishop of Canterbury, the Bishops of Winchester, Ely, Norwich, and St. David's ; and Alexius, Papal legate to the Church of Scotland. The remains were subsequently enclosed in a chest ornamented with gold and precious stones, which in its turn was placed in an elaborately carved shrine. In 1289 the shrine was replaced by another even more elaborate, " near the same spot in which it was formerly placed." The ceremony on this occasion was attended by the Bishop of Salisbury and the Duke of Cornwall. The shrine was destroyed early in the sixteenth century. It was not until 1870 that considerable portions of the second shrine were discovered, which are now to be seen, probably in their original position, in the Lady Chapel. According to Mr. W. H. Fairbairns " the shrine is the earliest example in England of natural foliage in architecture."

" The priory," says a writer in the " Victoria History of the Counties of England," " was never a distinguished place, it produced no remarkable men, and had more than its share of disorders and scandals." There was frequent trouble between the prior and the brethren and the municipal authorities of the city. In January 1423 the Bishop of Lincoln, we read, issued injunctions after a visitation of the monastery that the excessive and " voluptuous " expenses that had impoverished the house were to cease.

Wolsey is known to have accompanied Queen Katherine on her visit to the shrine of St. Frideswide in 1520, and, says Mrs. Dorothea Hamilton Fyfe * in her volume on Oxford, " perhaps for the first time it occurred to him how admirably situated was the Saint's church with its surrounding meadows and its proximity to the new foundation of Corpus and the old colleges of Merton and Oriel." Four years later we find Wolsey taking action to fulfil his long promise to bestow on Oxford a lasting mark of his esteem. " As a preparatory step † (and, probably, with a view of rendering the projected establishment independent of his own personal fortunes) he procured bulls from the Pope for the suppression of several priories and nunneries, which together yielded an annual revenue of nearly £2000. An income of this amount

---

* " Oxford " (Treasure House Series). By Dorothea Hamilton Fyfe.
† " The Beauties of England and Wales." J. N. Brewer.

74

CHRIST CHURCH (OXFORD): WATCHING CHAMBER OF THE SHRINE OF
ST. FRIDESWIDE

CHRIST CHURCH (OXFORD): CHAPTER HOUSE DOORWAY

he was authorised, by letter patent from the King, to settle on his new institution, to which he gave the name of Cardinal College, and the building of which he commenced on the site of an ancient priory dedicated to St. Frideswide. The original design of Wolsey was extensive beyond precedent. The Society was to consist of 160 persons, the chief of whom were to be engaged in the study of the sciences, divinity, canon and civil law, the arts, physics, and polite literature. Divine service was to be continually performed ; and he had collected the best architects of the age to project a concentration of beauties in the arrangement of the buildings. But before these grand intentions could be carried into effect the Cardinal experienced disgrace ; and the revenues bestowed by Wolsey, together with the incomplete portions of building raised under his inspection, were pathetically consigned by him to the fostering clemency of the King."

Antony à Wood, whom Mr. Andrew Lang considered to be " a scholar of a sort who had never been very common in Oxford ; he was a perfect dungeon of books," writing of St. Frideswide's Church, said : " After it came into the hands of Cardinal Wolsey, the west end thereof, containing almost half the body of the Church, was by him pulled down, intending that the remaining part should serve only for private prayers, and certain theological exercises. He caused also to be made over the Choir a fair carved roof of stone, and over the Church another of wood. . . . As for the solemnizing of greater service, and the delivery of sermons (publicly to the University, as it hath been reported), the Cardinal intended to have them done in the large church on the north side of the Quadrangle ; the foundation of which he had laid." *

Henry VIII had intended Oseney Abbey to be the head of the new Diocesan See, but his spendthrift character produced certain needs which led him to reduce this Abbey and to transfer the Bishop's stool to St. Frideswide's, which became the Cathedral Church of Christ in Oxford of Henry VIII's foundation with Robert King as first Bishop of Oxford. Wolsey had intended to build a magnificent chapel ; but Mrs. Fyfe reminds us " that the great church never rose above its foundations ; the King, who supplanted the Cardinal as patron, was no royal saint to create for his students a Tudor Cathedral of the dimensions of King's College Chapel at Cambridge. Henry VIII considered the small Priory Church quite good enough for his white-robed scholars, out of keeping though it was with the towering hall and the vast open space of the quadrangle. No sixteenth-century church can for a moment shine in comparison with this tiny Norman cathedral, endearingly irregular and rich in the fancies and architectural experiments of twelve centuries." When Queen Elizabeth visited Oxford in 1592 she heard a *Te Deum* sung in the Cathedral ; while in 1605 James I attended a service in the church, standing beneath a gorgeous canopy carried by Doctors of Divinity. Charles I and his queen in 1636 " went with all the lords to the Cathedral."

---

* " The History and Antiquities of the Colleges and Halls in the University of Oxford." Antony à Wood, M.A., 1668.

According to Wood, the Cathedral continued as Cardinal Wolsey had left it until 1630, when the then Dean and Chapter, " being minded to adorn it," made a number of alterations, " in the doing of all of which the workmen took up many monumental stones of marble, having most of them Saxon inscriptions engraven on them, which being looked upon by the Dean and Canons as old superfluous stuff, and unhandsome to be mixed with their new pavement, did cause them to be thrown out of the Church. . . . Which act of theirs, though it was for the decency of the Church, yet it cannot but be taken by many as sacrilegious, and in no wise to have been done by scholars and especially men of the Clergy."

However, there still exists in Christ Church an important link with Saxon times. At the eastern end of the Lady Chapel are three Saxon arches, of rude workmanship, which are considered by some authorities to be part of the convent founded by Didan, the father of St. Frideswide. Some students of Saxon architecture, however, place the apses at a date between 800 and the Conquest. On the exterior side of the wall in the Canons' Garden are the foundation of three apses discovered in 1887, corresponding with the arches, while another has been traced between them, so that in this wall we may have the remains of the small Saxon church with its eastward triple-apsidal termination.

Among the many literary contributions on Christ Church there is one by Mr. E. A. Greening Lamborn (" The History of Architecture in Oxford Stone "), in the course of which he says :

" We have in our own Cathedral a building that illustrates as well as any in England the passing of Romanesque architecture into Gothic. The chancel was begun in 1160, and the west end of the nave in 1180. Richard I, who lived as a child at Beaumont Palace, may well have been taken to see the builders at work on the new church of St. Frideswide. . . . East of the tower every arch is semicircular, the piers are ponderous, and the vault-ribs are massive ; but in the nave, though the main arches are round, the heads above are pointed and so are the arches of the aisle-vaults, the piers are less massive, and the vaulting ribs are light and thin, and their surface is relieved by grooves and ridges (moulding) carved in stone."

The beauty of the Choir is at once apparent to the visitor, who will be impressed by the exquisitely wrought Tudor ceiling, with its fan-tracery, supported by the massive Norman pillars. There are few roofs which outrival it. The delicate artistic work is probably that of the artificers employed by Wolsey. Within the arches of the Choir an arcade forms the Triforium.

Much of the present beauty of the Choir is due to the restoration of the eastern end by Sir Gilbert Scott, a task carried out in complete harmony with the earlier work, consisting of a fine rose

Tom Tower from
St. Aldate's Street

window, below which is an arcade and two other windows. The reredos is richly gilded and composed of sandstone and Rosso Antico. North of the Choir is the Lady Chapel, its delicate shafts contrasting with the earlier massive piers. The nave roof is sixteenth-century work. In the south aisle is the memorial to John King, last Abbot of Oseney and first Bishop of Oxford, with the window by the Dutch artist Abraham van Linge (1630), showing King in his episcopal robes, and Oseney Abbey in the background. The Latin Chapel (so called because prayers used to be read in Latin there daily), dedicated to St. Catherine, patroness of Learning, contains carved woodwork of Wolsey's time, and has a fifteenth-century watching chamber for St. Frideswide's shrine, richly constructed in stone and wood ; it is also noted for its beautiful stained-glass windows. The chapel is generally attributed to the Lady Elizabeth Montacute, to whom the Priory owed Christ Church meadow.

The small cloisters on the south side of the cathedral date from 1499 and are the gift of Sherborne, Dean of St. Paul's, who rebuilt the entire cloister out of pity for the condition in which he found the Canons. Above the cloisters, to the south, can be seen the Old Library, at one time the refectory, which is now occupied by undergraduates. An ornate Norman doorway, attributed to Prior Guimond, on the eastern side leads to the Chapter House. In the eastern wall of this is preserved the foundation-stone of Wolsey's school at Ipswich. When the Angevin kings lived at Beaumont Palace, Parliament frequently met in this perfect specimen of thirteenth-century Gothic. From the Chapter House visitors can pass beneath the Belfry Tower to the grand staircase, notable for its fan-tracery, into Christ Church hall.

Bishop King's Monument

Thus we leave the Cathedral Church of Christ, in the chancel of which Cranmer heard the mock Papal sentence upon himself—and suffered degradation at the hands of Bonner in the Cloisters—where Charles I gave thanks to God for his few victories, and where Dr. Pusey rests. The visitor will doubtless pass under Tom Tower, a part of the splendid work for Christ Church by Oxford's famous Bishop, John Fell (1676–1686), and one of the three buildings by Wren in Oxford, with its seven-ton bell from Oseney Abbey, which nightly rings its signal of 101 strokes for the closing of the colleges.

77

ST. WOOLOS (NEWPORT, MON.)

T. WOOLOS CHURCH, which occupies a commanding site in the industrial town of Newport (Mon.), and is one of the most interesting buildings—ecclesiastically, architecturally, and historically—in the Principality of Wales, is now the Pro-Cathedral of the newly created diocese of Monmouth. The diocese, formed in 1921, is almost conterminous with Monmouthshire.

St. Woolos derives its name from Gwynlliw Filwr (or Woolos the Warrior) who succeeded his father Glewys, the first chieftain of Gwent after the departure of the Romans in 412. Woolos married Gwladys, the daughter of a Brecknockshire chieftain, and one of his eleven sons, Cadoc " the Wise," brought about the conversion of his parents to Christianity.

On Stow Hill in the early part of the sixth century Woolos erected a chapel, the predecessor of the present Pro-Cathedral. The little chapel, believed to be of mud and wattle, was replaced by a larger building, and then by one even more extensive, until St. Mary's Chapel was erected for which has been claimed the distinction of being perhaps the oldest building for Christian worship in the kingdom. There is, however, some doubt as to the accuracy of the stages of growth mentioned.

In his short history of St. Woolos Church, the Archdeacon of Monmouth (the Ven. D. H. Griffiths, M.A.), says : " When we contemplate the days of St. Woolos we are carried back to a period anterior to the coming of the Norman, and even of the Saxon, when Britain after having been evacuated by the Romans who held dominion for 350 years in the island, was left in the hand of the British or Welsh people who had been conquered and subjugated by the Romans in the middle of the first century. What we have to realise is that the founder and builder of the first church on this spot had been dead nearly a hundred years before the coming of St. Augustine to Kent for the conversion of the pagan Saxons."

The church of St. Woolos has a Norman Nave, commenced some fifty years after the Battle of Hastings, of which Prof. E. A. Freeman said " No better or more typical Norman interior on a moderate scale could be desired." In the thirteenth century the church was added to, but some of the work was swept away during the enlargement round about 1440. Then the north and south aisles were built in the Gothic style, and so beautiful are they that the interior of the church has been described as " a Norman jewel in a Gothic casket." The massive square tower, built by Jasper Tudor, Duke of Bedford, is of the time of Henry VII. In 1854 the church was extensively restored. Archdeacon Griffiths remarks that " up to that time the chancel had for a considerable period been shut off from the rest of the church by a great blank wall, and used merely as a charnel house. This wall was pierced,

78

ST. WOOLOS (NEWPORT, MON.): THE INTERIOR

ST. WOOLOS (NEWPORT, MON.): NORMAN ARCHES

and the present chancel arch inserted. The chancel itself was thoroughly restored, being made once again an integral part of the building. Several new features were introduced to the detriment, as we judge to-day, of the thirteenth-century structure. For example, the present east window was inserted in the place of a beautiful fifteenth-century window, and the sculptured corbels on either side of the wall fixed. These corbels are not in line, but bob up and down in a fussy kind of way, offending the eye." The Archdeacon adds that " the restoration of 1854 was, for the period, a most excellently carried out scheme." In 1913 the church was again restored, and the stripping of the matchboarding from the roofs brought to light the fine fifteenth-century oak rafters. By the removal of the fanlight and folding doors from the Norman arch in St. Mary's Chapel, the two buildings were thrown into one. "This arch, or doorway," wrote Prof. Freeman, "is perhaps, on the whole, the most remarkable architectural example in the district. It is a superb example of Romanesque of a character by no means usual in England."

A striking feature of the ancient building is the small low building between the Tower and the main portion of the Church usually called St. Mary's Chapel. This part of the Church has ever been an enigma to all who have studied it, nor has its position as yet ever been satisfactorily explained or accounted for.

The archway leading from St. Mary's into St. Woolos is remarkable from the fact that though the mouldings of the arch are Norman, and very fine, the detached columns which support them are Roman, and probably brought from some Roman remains at Caerleon, situated three miles up the river Usk, and during the Roman occupation a city of front rank importance. These columns with their floriated capitals are worthy of inspection and study, particularly the rude carvings on the two exposed sides of each of the Corinthian capitals.

The subject-matter of the grotesque but vigorous sculptures appear to be a representation in four consecutive scenes of the Noachian Deluge.

Of the thirteenth-century craftsmanship there remain the chancel, the Leper window on the level of the chancel floor within the altar rails, the three-light window in the Crindau Chapel, the two windows, one on each side of the chancel, in the nave, formed to light the pre-Reformation rood loft, a two-light window above the pulpit, and remnants of the chancel arch.

Behind the pulpit steps is the Hagioscope, or Squint, which enabled worshippers to see the High Altar from the North Aisle. Above the organ is to be seen the entrance to the Rood Loft. The south wall of the South Aisle contains a fifteenth-century piscina.

All that exists to-day of the ancient tombs and monuments are the mutilated effigies and fragments deposited in the quaint recesses in St. Mary's Chapel. The headless figure in the niche in the Tower is the effigy of Jasper Tudor, the builder of the Tower.

For wellnigh fifteen hundred years the County of Monmouth had formed an integral part of the ancient Diocese of Llandaff. After the Disestablishment of the Church in Wales, the Governing Body of " The Church in Wales," on

79

September 28, 1921, ordered the creation of a new Diocese for the territory comprised within the Archdeaconry of Monmouth, and for the purpose of carrying out this order decreed that, " *On and after the eighteenth of October, 1921, the area contained within the existing boundaries of the Archdeaconry of Monmouth shall cease to be part of the Diocese of Llandaff and shall become and thenceforth be a separate episcopal Diocese to be called the Diocese of Monmouth.*"

The Electoral College for the first time in its existence met in the Pro-Cathedral Church of St. Woolos, Newport, on Friday, November 18, 1921, for the purpose of electing the first Bishop of the recently created See.

The Venerable Charles Alfred Green, D.D., Archdeacon of Monmouth, was duly elected. He was consecrated in the Cathedral Church of Llandaff on St. Thomas's Day, December 21, 1921, by the Archbishop of Wales, the Bishops of Llandaff, St. David's, Bangor, Winchester, and Norwich, and Bishop Crossley, and enthroned in the Pro-Cathedral Church of St. Woolos, Newport, on January 3, 1922. The Bishop signs " C. Monemuten," " Monemuten " being the abbreviated form of the adjective " Monemutensis " and is derived from " Monemuta," the Latin equivalent of Monmouth. The Diocese is co-extensive with the County of Monmouth, having a population of nearly half a million.

Although the County of Monmouth for fifteen centuries was included in the Diocese of Llandaff, the Church of St. Woolos was given, at a very early period, to the Abbey of Gloucester, and probably the small but perfect Norman Nave was built by the Abbot and monks of that Monastery.

The Church and its lands remained in its possession until the dissolution of the monasteries, when on the erection of the new Bishopric of Gloucester in the reign of Henry VIII, the right of presentation, patronage, etc., were vested in the Bishop of Gloucester, with whom they remained until the episcopate of the late Bishop Lewis of Llandaff, who, effecting an exchange of benefices with the Diocese of Gloucester, selected the Rev. W. Conybeare Bruce, M.A., afterwards Archdeacon of Monmouth, to be the first vicar appointed by a Welsh bishop.

Whatever claims Monmouthshire may have to be an English County, ecclesiastically, as well as topographically, it is, as it always has been, an inalienable part of Wales, and Welsh Churchmen rejoiced when the Mother Parish of Newport was restored to Llandaff, and is to-day the premier parish in the Diocese of Monmouth.

LLANDAFF CATHEDRAL: THE WEST FRONT

LLANDAFF CATHEDRAL: THE REREDOS

LLANDAFF CATHEDRAL

LANDAFF, with its Cathedral the possessor of the longest unbroken tradition in the religious life of the British Isles, has a tranquillity which reminds one of Wells. While practically a suburb of Cardiff, the principal centre of business life in Wales, Llandaff retains a peculiar charm and interest which is all its own. It is little more than a village city, in the centre of which and among green fields at the foot of a ridge rising abruptly from the Taff valley stands the shrine of SS. Dubricius and Teilo; not surrounded by a Cathedral Close, though a modern Deanery overlooks the Western Door with the ruined gateway of the old Bishop's Palace on the south-east, a memorial to the ruthlessness of Owen Glendower.

Llandaff is another of the early ecclesiastical cities traditionally associated with the name of the British King Lucius, by whom a church is said to have been built there in A.D. 180. Some support for this tradition may be drawn from the fact that the little city on the Taff is not far removed from the famous City of the Legions on the Usk (Caerleon) where, according to legend, sat some 1750 years ago one of the first three Archbishops of the British Church, a statement which few historians, however, accept.

The late Mr. George Thomas Clark, whose opinion finds a fitting place in this volume because of his associations with the Great Western Railway, he having worked with Brunel at Paddington and on the erection of the bridges over the Thames at Basildon and Moulsford, wrote in his scholarly volumes on *Cartæ et Alia Munimenta quæ ad Dominium de Glamorgan pertinent*:

"The history of Glamorgan is not alone to be deduced from its topographical or philological remains. The bright light of Christianity shone early upon its shores, and created, as was usually the case, a literature of its own. The Welsh remember with justifiable pride that their acceptance of the doctrines of the Gospel long preceded, and was independent of, the mission of Augustine and the foundation of the Province of Canterbury ; and without absolutely subscribing to the claims of King Lucius to have received baptism from the Pope Eleutherius in the middle of the second century, there is reason to believe that the faith in Christ had been not only preached, but had had time to be infected with the Pelagian heresy, to extirpate which missionaries from Brittany, led by Germanius and Lupus, found their way here as early as the fourth century. It was under their teaching that Dubricius founded the See of Llandaff. . . . The boundaries of that See are by much the oldest of our local limitaries, and have remained almost unchanged from twelve to fourteen centuries. . . . The Cathedral of Llandaff is probably the earliest ecclesiastical foundation in Britain, and the actual structure, though, of course, later by several centuries, contains some excellent twelfth-century work. Also with the Church at Llandaff are closely connected some of the earliest and most valuable Welsh historical records. The 'Llyfr Teilo,' or 'Liber Landavensis,' though compiled probably in its present form under Bishop Urban in the twelfth century, is certainly based on an older record, and includes several grants by Welsh princes, throwing original and unquestionable light upon the early ecclesiastical topography of the See, its religious foundations, and upon the lives of the most eminent of the many holy men who have adorned its annals."

Before retiring to Bardsey Island, Dubricius, Llandaff's first bishop, handed over his foundation to Teilo (*circa* 540). Thenceforward Llandaff steadily grew in importance. Urban, the thirtieth bishop of the diocese, rebuilt the Cathedral, which forms a considerable part of the present structure, dedicating it in 1120 to St. Peter, St. Dubricius, St. Teilo, and St. Oudoceus. Bishop Godwin, in his " Catalogue of Bishops," dealing with the rebuilding by Urban, says : " The Archbishop (of Canterbury) the rather to draw on the liberality of men in contributing towards the building of the church took upon him to release a fourth part of all penance inflicted unto such as should bestow anything towards the same. By that means having gathered the summes of money, he began the building of the Church, which now standeth, April 14th, 1120 ; and having finished it built anew also the houses belonging to it." In 1187 Archbishop Baldwin, and his chaplain, Giraldus Cambrensis, preached the Crusade at Llandaff, the spot being marked by a cross, which was restored in 1897.

From the time of Henry III the Cathedral passed through many vicissitudes. Owen Glendower did considerable damage to the Bishop's residence. According to another writer, after the reign of Henry VIII the See, largely through the alienations of its bishops and the depredations of the canons, became impoverished and the Cathedral gradually lapsed into a state of ruin. So it remained for a long period. Cattle roamed over the churchyard, and boys played games amongst the tombs in the Nave—marbles are mentioned as one of the pastimes. In fact, the decay became so great that the removal of the See to Cardiff was discussed early in the eighteenth century. The south-west tower had become a mere skeleton of its former self, parts of other towers had fallen and the Nave was no longer suitable for Divine Service, which was continued in the Lady Chapel. From 1732 to 1752 an attempt was made, by the conversion of the Choir, Presbytery, and a portion of the Nave into an " Italian Temple," to give more accommodation to worshippers. Happily the work of the builder did not destroy the main features of the building. So dangerous had the south-western tower become in 1786 that it was pulled down. In 1836, however, a restoration scheme was initiated and was continued by Bishop Ollivant as the outcome of which a large portion of the Cathedral assumed its pristine beauty. Choral services were resumed in 1857, and during the next twelve years the western portion of the Nave and the south-western tower were completed. The restoration was carried out under the superintendence of Mr. John Pritchard, architect, of Llandaff.

The most striking exterior feature of the Cathedral is the long, unbroken body, comprising under an uninterrupted roof, Nave, Choir, and Presbytery, with the large Lady Chapel (1265–87) projecting from the east end at a slightly lower elevation. The absence of a central tower is noticeable, but is more than compensated for by the two western towers. That on the north, built by Jasper Tudor, uncle of Henry VII, being of the Somerset type, resembles the tower of St. John's Church, Cardiff. The south-west tower and spire, which rises to a height of 195 feet, and is considered to be one of the best pieces of modern architecture, was designed by Mr. John Pritchard. The west front possesses a number of points of beauty. Of the interior the features to be noticed are the plan of the piers sustaining the roof, the absence of a triforium, the Norman Choir arch built by Bishop Urban, and the peculiar form of the Chapter House, the lower storey of which is Early English. On the North side of the Cathedral there are two windows with stained glass, certainly by William Morris, and on the South one by Morris, and a very striking window, with the Crucifixion for subject, which was designed and executed by Silvestre Sparrow, of London. The reredos by Dante Gabriel Rossetti is famous, and the tomb of Dean Vaughan always attracts attention. The reputed tomb of St. Teilo is on the south side of the Presbytery, while that of St. Dubricius is on the north side, the relics having been translated to Llandaff by Bishop Urban in 1120. Among a number of ancient monuments is one to Sir David Mathew (1461), who was standard-bearer to Edward IV at the bloody battle between the Yorkists and Lancastrians on Towton Field.

Llandaff is symbolical of the continuity of the Church in Wales, for in its Cathedral, on St. Thomas's Day 1921, the first Bishop of the Disestablished Church in Wales, Dr. Green of Monmouth, was consecrated by the first Archbishop of the Province of Wales.

Tomb of Sir David Mathew

BRECON CATHEDRAL

ON a hill above the town of Brecon " north without the waulle upon the Ripe of Honddu," as Leland wrote, ſtands what was the fineſt parish church in Wales, dedicated to St. John the Evangeliſt, until June 1923, when it became the Cathedral church of the newly-created diocese of Swansea and Brecon. Both in size and architecture it has for years been the second moſt beautiful church in the Principality, being only exceeded by St. David's Cathedral. Professor Freeman considered St. John's to be " the nobleſt of a class of which a good many inſtances occur in Wales ; massive cruciform churches with central towers, whose high roof and gables invariably present a picturesque external outline. The leading idea is that of simple bulk. Brecon Priory impresses us more ſtrongly with the idea of general magnitude than many buildings of much greater positive dimensions. This is, perhaps, partly occasioned by its supreme simplicity of ſtructure. The ground plan consiſts of a nave with aisles, a north porch, a central tower or Choir, with transepts and an eaſtern limb forming a large presbytery without regular aisles, but with a remarkable arrangement of chapels on each side. The church was, doubtless, commenced not long after the foundation of the Priory, but probably the nave might not be completed till towards the middle of the twelfth century. The choir, transepts, and presbytery were rebuilt during the thirteenth century, the fourteenth gradually transformed the Norman nave into a Decorated building. The ſtyle of the presbytery is common Early English, extremely good, but not remarkable for richness ; in the exterior, indeed, remarkably the reverse."

The dimensions of the Cathedral are : Nave, length 107 feet, breadth 34 feet 6 inches ; square of Lantern, 34 feet 6 inches ; Chancel, length 63 feet, breadth 29 feet ; Transepts, length 35 feet and 36 feet, breadth 28 feet ; total length 205 feet.

For many years it was known as the Priory Church, having been attached to the adjoining Benedictine Priory founded by Bernard Newmarch as a cell of Battle Abbey in Sussex, when having conquered this part of the country from the Welsh, he built the caſtle and town of Brecon. In mediæval times it was invariably called the " Church of the Holy Rood," a name which it retained to the middle of the sixteenth century on account of the many pilgrimages to the gigantic Rood in the church. It is the third sacred edifice built on this site. The firſt was taken down to make way for Bernard Newmarch's Norman church, built for the repose of the soul of William the Conqueror. The only remains of Newmarch's church are the font and the north and south walls in the nave immediately joining the weſtern arch of the tower. The present church was begun in the early part of the thirteenth century, the Early English chancel, transepts and tower being erected in the time of Giles de Breos, Bishop

BRECON CATHEDRAL

BRECON CATHEDRAL: INTERIOR

of Hereford (died 1215), and of his brother Reginald (died 1228) who is the only Lord of Brecon buried here.

The Cathedral occupies a fine site above the town. When ascending the hill the visitor sees the embattled walls and gateway of the monastery, the old barn and its curious gargoyles, and a fine figure of St. John the Baptist holding an Agnus Dei built into the wall. Passing through the beautiful modern lych gate a very fine view of the exterior of the Cathedral is obtained, the large dormer window rising from the aisle roof forming a picturesque feature in the noble massive outline which the whole presents.

Near the porch are two of the largest known stone stoups, found buried in the Cloister Garth, whilst on the right, on entering the Cathedral, is the broken fragment of the holy water stoup in its original position.

The nave was built in the fourteenth century when the de Bohuns were owners of the Lordship, and the wide span of the arches and the simplicity of its detail contribute to its grandeur.

Until the chapels at the east were erected, the ground plan formed a perfect cross, as was usual in monastic churches. The whole of the building east of the nave formed the Monks' Church, and the nave and its aisles were used as a parish church. The squint, still in the south wall of the nave opening from the dormitory of the guest-house of the monastery, enabled the pilgrims resting there to see the Rood in the dimly-lighted church. The windows of the nave are Decorated of a type general in Herefordshire, as are the clerestory windows, but their position is unusual as they are placed over the pillars instead of over the arches. In the nave are sepulchral slabs placed there for preservation ; those incised with crosses and trade emblems are in many respects unique. The recumbent effigy carved in wood of a lady, one of the Gameses of Aberbran (*circa* 1555), is worthy of close attention, as is the remarkable cresset-stone formerly used for lighting the church, which is the largest yet discovered. The stone of which the Cathedral is built is the old red sandstone of a beautiful colour obtained from a quarry in the neighbouring Priory Groves. The history of the building is written on its walls in a remarkable manner, so that those who look may read it for themselves.

One of the most impressive features of the building is the massive tower with its great arches, where the Early English work begins.

The north transept or Battle Chapel obtains its name from being used until recent years as the burial place of the inhabitants of the hamlet of Battle, named after the celebrated Abbey in Sussex. Two arches lead from this transept into the Havard Chapel.

The glory of the Cathedral is the Choir, which, combining perfect simplicity and purity of detail with massive

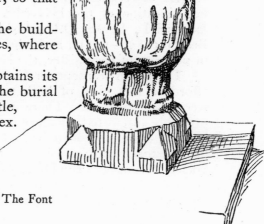

The Font

proportions, is thoroughly representative of the plainer phase of Early English work. Stern and grim as is its outside appearance, the interior has a loveliness of its own which is unsurpassed ; Freeman considered it " one of the choicest examples of the Early English style." The chancel consists of four bays ; it was intended to be vaulted, but, beyond the erection of the vaulting shafts and springers, the design was not carried out until the restoration in 1862, when the now beautiful roof completed the unfinished work begun 650 years before. The chapel on the south, supposed to be the lost chapel dedicated to St. Lawrence, and now used as a vestry by the clergy, contains many sculptured stones of great interest collected from various parts of the building. North of the altar is a most curious stone let into the pavement, bearing a representation of the rood (very much defaced) with four monks kneeling beneath. This is supposed to have been the altar-piece.

The East window is filled with stained glass to the memory of the officers and men of the South Wales Borderers (24th Regiment), of whom 21 officers and 590 men were killed in action on the field of Isandhlwana or in the defence of Rorke's Drift, 1879 ; and brass tablets on the north wall commemorate the names of those who gave their lives for Queen and Country in one of the bravest of British regiments, possessing as it does the second largest number of V.C.'s (twenty-two) in the infantry regiments.

The Havard Chapel, so called from having been enlarged by the powerful Norman family of that name whose burial place it was, has been restored and beautified to the memory of the 311 officers and 5466 men of the South Wales Borderers who gave their lives in the Great War, 1914–18. The ornaments and furniture as well as the stained-glass windows were given as individual memorials. On the altar is placed the Roll of Honour, and in front of it are the Houseling Benches, which formerly stood in the chancel. Above the altar is a fine painting given by the late Captain Graystone. In an archway in the south wall is the squint through which is given a view of the high altar. The floor is paved with memorial stones, some of great interest. To be seen in the north-east corner of this chapel is a slab bearing the recumbent effigies of Walter Aubrey of Abercynrig (died 1312) and his wife. The beautification of the Havard Chapel was carried out under the Right Rev. Edward L. Bevan, D.D., Bishop of Swansea and Brecon, who was vicar of Brecon (1897–1921), and who with his family restored the Corvizors' Chapel in memory of their sister, the late Miss Bevan.

The south transept, or Capel-y-Cochiad (Chapel of the Red-haired Men), affords a fine view of both transepts and the tower. The red-haired men were the Normans. There are corbels in the corner above the stairs which probably supported a gallery commanding a view into the church and opening into the Monks' Dormitory. One of the chapels on the east side has recently been restored and furnished by the members of the Church of England Men's Society throughout the Diocese, and it will be associated with work among men and boys. The other is occupied by the organ. On the west wall is a fine piece of sculpture by Flaxman to the memory of Mr. James (died 1789). The arch on the west of the transept gives an entrance into the south aisle of the nave, and through an open door which was the monks' entrance from the Cloisters can be seen the Cloister Garth, now the private grounds of the Priory House (King Charles I slept here on the night of August 5, 1645).

In the Corvizors' Chapel at the east of the north aisle is an interesting recumbent effigy of a layman (*circa* 1350) who may have been the builder of the nave, and whose chantry chapel this probably was. The graceful dormer window above contains figures in stained glass of the Founders of the Faith in the parish, whilst that below has the Builders of its Churches. The stairs in the walls north and south of the nave leading to the arched doors which open on the rood-loft are very interesting, as well as the stone corbels above, on which the rood-beams rest. Until the restoration of 1874 these stairs and doorways were covered with plaster and whitewash, and their existence was unknown.

On April 23, 1862, the Choir, Transepts, and Tower were reopened after their restoration by Sir Gilbert Scott, who also restored the Nave and its aisles in 1874–75. The whole work was begun and completed by the late Rev. Prebendary Garnons Williams, of Abercamlais, and the late Rev. Prebendary Herbert Williams, who were successively vicars of Brecon. St. John's is a worthy addition to the Cathedrals of England and Wales, for, although the youngest Diocesan Church, it preserves the phases of the glorious work of the Early builders. The reader who is desirous of inspecting St. John's should obtain a copy of " Brecon Cathedral," a brochure compiled by Miss G. E. F. Morgan, J.P. of that city and churchwarden of St. John's (1920–22), upon which this account is mainly founded, and which is on sale in the Cathedral.

Brecon itself is a place of great antiquity. Caer Bannau, the Roman Bannium, said to have been entrenched by Ostorius Scapula (A.D. 54), is two miles away. From the stone of Bannium Bernard de Newmarch commenced to build Brecon Castle, very little of which now remains. In the Ely Tower Morton, Bishop of Ely, conspired to overthrow Richard III. St. Mary's Church dates from the eleventh century. Christ's College, which stands on the site of a Dominican Friary, and was founded by Henry VIII, has a fine Early English Chapel.

ST. DAVID'S CATHEDRAL

"That marvellous Cathedral of St. David's, in its secluded basin at the very extremity of the land, shut out from the world and enclosed as within a natural sanctuary, with its craggy coast and headland and island, and glistening shore and purple cliff, every spring and bay and inlet teeming with some strange legend of those primitive days of David and Non and Teilo."—Dean Stanley.

THOSE who visit the ancient "village-city" of St. David's will feel as the celebrated Dean felt when he wrote the sentence given above ; for this sentence perhaps, more fittingly than any other, describes the setting in which this gem of Cathedrals reposes. That great scholar, historian, and Bishop of St. David's (Connop Thirlwall) wrote : "In St. David's Cathedral, Wales is in possession of an Architectural Monument almost unique in this country—a treasure of Mediæval Architecture, to which there are few parallels or equals throughout the length and breadth of this land." Had Bishop Thirlwall been living to-day, when so much of the glory of St. David's has been recovered as the outcome of patient and devoted labours during the past thirty years, he would have written *unique* instead of "almost unique"—for St. David's is unique.

The Cathedral Church of St. Andrew and St. David's appears to the visitor most unexpectedly, after a journey across miles of wild, sparsely populated country, with glimpses of the Atlantic and wondrous rocky coast-line. At last the one long street of St. David's—it has only five streets—is reached ; and just past the ancient cross a square embattled edifice, storm-beaten and grey with an age of nearly 750 years, and apparently springing from nowhere, comes suddenly into view. It proves to be nothing less than the magnificent Cathedral, standing at the foot of the broad staircase of the "Thirty-nine Articles." To describe the scene is difficult, so weirdly desolate, yet so profoundly beautiful, is this deep dell below the last of the four thirteenth-century gateways which gives access to the Close. There stands the Cathedral from which William Laud exercised episcopal rule prior to his promotion to Canterbury. It is a living Pompeii—a lasting memorial to the glories of the age which gave Wales such prelate-architects as Henry de Gower, such buildings as St. Mary's College and Chapel, and an Episcopal palace, sufficiently capacious to accommodate the occupant of every See in Europe, with its graceful open parapet and exquisite traceried wheel-window, one of the finest specimens of domestic architecture in Great Britain. And for a background is stern-faced craggy Carn Llidi, north-west against the sky-line.

Beneath the old gateway, and viewing the noble Church which holds all that is human of St. David, the visitor pauses, and uppermost comes the question which must come to all who make this pilgrimage : Why is this Cathedral,

ST. DAVID'S CATHEDRAL

ST. DAVID'S CATHEDRAL: THE CHOIR

ST. DAVID'S CATHEDRAL: ROOF OF LANTERN TOWER

ST. DAVID'S CATHEDRAL: RUINS

Facing page 89

with these remarkable ruins speaking of a one-time dominating power, here in this far-away westernmost portion of Wales ?

For some part of the answer to that question we can reasonably turn to the " History of St. David's " * by the late Canon (afterwards Archdeacon) W. L. Bevan, M.A. " It is just as if the Cathedral of Exeter Diocese," he writes, " had been planted on the Land's End of Cornwall, with this difference, however, that St. David's is farther away from any considerable centre of population than a cathedral on the Land's End would be. These peculiarities occasionally give rise to the question how the Cathedral came to be placed in such an unsuitable position. The question rather assumes that the Diocese was first formed and the site of the Cathedral afterwards selected. In point of fact the reverse is the case. The Church of St. David's preceded the Diocese of St. David's. The former was founded as a monastic church in a spot which would be recognised by all as admirably adapted by its surroundings for the seclusion of a monastery. From being a purely monastic church it grew, probably by a gradual process, into a Diocesan church with the principality of Dyfed (the *Demetia* of Latin writers), comprising Pembrokeshire, with the adjacent parts of Carmarthenshire and Cardiganshire as its area. Once installed in that position its influence extended with that of Dyfed, and to this circumstance we may perhaps attribute its absorption in the eighth century of the adjacent diocese of Llanbadarn, which occupied the northern portions of Cardiganshire and Radnorshire. The growth of the diocese was from West to East."

Archdeacon Bevan does not agree with the view that the establishment of a See at St. David's was the outcome of a movement East to West with a starting-point at Caerleon, but believes that it was due " to causes internal to Wales itself and particularly to a great civil or dynastic revolution which occurred shortly before the period of its foundation." The significance of the phrase " East to West " will be appreciated after the pilgrim has carefully studied much of the history told by the Cathedral itself. Before Augustine came St. David's was.

Old legends tell that St. Patrick founded on the slopes of Carn Llidi a missionary college, known as " Ty Gwyn," or the " White House." It is known that after St. Patrick's death in 465 Irish missionaries came to Wales for instruction. To this day there are roads in the district known as St. Patrick's roads. In the autumn of 1924 Mr. Francis Green and Mr. A. B. Badger discovered the actual foundations of St. Patrick's chapel with ruins of the old Altar in a field close to White Sand Bay, and near the " White House," about a mile from St. David's Head. Inside the juncture of the western and southern walls was found a skull, afterwards considered by Dr. Fleure, Professor of Anthropology at the University College of Wales, Aberystwyth, to be that of a very old man. Other human remains were also unearthed. Mr. W. D. Caroë, the well-known architect, is of opinion that the chapel is pre-mediæval, and was erected between the fifth and tenth centuries. Among the Celtic holy

---

* " Diocesan Histories : St. David's." S.P.C.K.

men and women educated there was a Welsh princess Non, daughter of Cynyr of Caer Gawch, a powerful chieftain. To " Ty Gwyn " David, the son of Non, was sent, and because of his piety he was trained as a priest by the holy St. Illtyd. Cynyr we are told gave his estate to David, on which the latter founded a sanctuary for men of all tribes and nationalities, and to mark the boundaries he had a deep trench dug, which to-day is known as Monk's Dyke. That the sanctuary was for " all tribes and all nationalities " must have been remembered by those who placed the statues of St. Patrick (Ireland), St. David (Britain), and St. Denis (Gaul) in the niches on the left side of the Rood Screen of the Cathedral— probably the only Cathedral in the world representing international Christianity. In this sanctuary David erected his church, the first of the three predecessors of the jewel-like Cathedral which stands to-day in the valley of the Alan—the *Vallis Rosina*, the valley of the Roses. Here, within a short distance of Roman Menevia or Manapia (Mynyw), grew Ty Dewi or St. David's.

If we do not care to accept legend there is good authority for the belief that sometimes after A.D. 530 David made the site of the present Cathedral the chief seat of the British Church in South Wales, a church known to have had a vigorous life for nearly two hundred years before that time. Mr. Herbert M. Vaughan, F.S.A.,* says : " The dread of an imminent Anglo-Saxon invasion of Gwent, the determination to remove his monastic clergy from court influence, and the desire of opening closer communications with the sister Churches of Ireland, are among the various reasons suggested for David's remarkable policy which made St. David's the leading religious centre in South Wales for nearly a thousand years." The great personality of David, a born leader of men, strong in warfare, of abiding piety, must have attracted a great many followers to him during his earliest years when he founded monas- teries at Glastonbury, Bath and elsewhere, thus creating the nucleus for the Christianising movement which derived much of its motive power from Menevia. Mungo, the Irishman who was driven from the bishopric of Strathclyde, stayed for a time with St. David at Menevia, and founded a monastery at Llanelwy which he handed over to St. Asaph, after whom it became named. Finian of Leinster passed under St. David his earlier years, and when he returned to Ireland took with him Britons who assisted him to found Clontard monastery, of which he was the first Abbot.† Finian preached to Mercia and to the East Saxons.

Fourteen hundred years of history seem bridged over as the pilgrim enters the Cathedral wherein are the remains of St. David and his faithful henchman, St. Justinian. It was from here, to quote from an article [describing a recent visit which he had paid to St. David's] in the *Welsh Outlook* for March 1923 by Mr. J. A. Price, M.A., that in the days of Sulien and Rhygyvarch "the last free voices of Dewisland were raised against the nearing menace of the Latin crozier and Norman lance. The protest failed, and even the

---

* " Encyclopædia Britannica," XIth Edition.
† " The First Twelve Centuries of British Story." J. W. Jeudwine (1912).

EXETER

ST. DAVID'S

LLANDAFF

ST. WOOLOS (MON.)

BRECON

TRURO.

CATHEDRALS" (G.W.R.)

genius and chivalry of Giraldus could not win back the lost liberties. So for seven hundred weary years Menevia sat on her rocks, a dethroned princess, whose crown Canterbury had torn from her brows. To-day, in the Nave of the Cathedral, one sees the Welsh flag. It was put there, indeed, to honour the victims of recent wars, but what would the old Anglicizers of the past—Dean Davey, or even Professor Freeman—have thought of the presence of the Red Dragon? But more impressive to the historical sense was the new bust of Giraldus Cambrensis in the Vaughan Chapel, crowned with the laurel leaf and with the mitre lying below. Certainly it was a strange co-incidence that Giraldus' bust should have appeared in the Cathedral immediately after the severance of the Welsh Church from the English State. Giraldus has returned to his Cathedral to enjoy a posthumous victory. The cause for which he fought has triumphed after a weary waiting of seven hundred years. But can one believe that the casket which Dean Williams shows really contains the bones of the Patron Saint of Wales? The Dean's case cannot be ignored. There is no doubt that the relics he possesses were regarded as genuine in the eleventh century, when Bernard the Norman came to the Vale of Roses. And the Normans, we must remember, took over the Cathedral from patriotic nationalists of the school of Sulien and Rhygyvarch, and through the whole of the Welsh period of St. David's business interests alone would have caused these relics to be preserved with the utmost care and devotion."

Visitors will wander at will amongst the many gems of Sculpture in the Cathedral which, as already stated, is the fourth church upon this site. That built by St. David was burned, A.D. 645; a similar fate overtook the second in 1088, and the third existed for nearly a century, when it was demolished to make way for the existing building erected by Bishop Peter de Leia, who came to St. David's after having been Prior of Wenlock. Of the work begun by Leia in 1180 there now remains the Nave, Transepts, Presbytery and part of the Central Tower. The Central Tower seems to have given some trouble from an early date, doubtless due to the cause discovered by Sir Gilbert Scott, who had charge of the restoration work commenced in 1862. Beneath the south-western pillar of the Tower he found a spring, believed to be " St. David's Well," which caused a subsidence. This spring has never been known to fail, even in the driest weather. In 1220 the Tower fell, and was at once rebuilt. It, however, required attention again during the episcopacy of Henry de Gower (1328–1347), the great builder and Chancellor of Oxford University. In 1862 Sir Gilbert Scott also strengthened the south-western pillar and inserted girders below the Lantern, thus rendering the Tower safe, though it is considered advisable still to take precautions. The absence of a peal of bells at St. David's is attributed to the desire of the old custodians of the Cathedral to reduce vibration in the tower to the minimum.

The great South Porch speaks through its quaint carving of the antiquity of the Cathedral. With some difficulty the visitor will be able to decipher immediately over the doorway what must have been a gem of sculpture in its pristine state, and before vandal hands disfigured it. On the left hand and right hand respectively can be seen the Tree of Adam and the Tree of Jesse, both culminating in a representation of Our Lord in Glory in the centre. Looking from the centre of the western end of the Nave through the Rood Screen to the High Altar, the pilgrim will notice the considerable rise of the church, until the floor of the sanctuary is on a level with the base of the great window, which fills half the space of the western wall. This slanting downwards from East to West is unique—even the pillars of the Nave are not perpendicular. This curious forward leaning cannot be attributed, as some ill-informed writers say, to the earthquake of 1248. A subsidence would have left gaping cracks, of which there are no signs. Rather is it that Leia designed his cruciform cathedral to a plan which symbolised the Saviour "upon the Cross, with head inclined," and which gave worshippers in the days prior to the stone Choir Screen an uninterrupted view of the High Altar from the extreme western limits of the building.

As the eye wanders round the Nave it takes in the strange combination of triforium and clerestory, also unique at St. David's. The triforium merges into the round-headed, richly ornamented clerestory—twin-pointed arches appearing with a circular opening between each pair. From these triumphs of architecture the pilgrim will turn to the marvellously rich and original flat ceiling of Irish oak, the gift of Treasurer Owen Pole (*circa* 1500). The arches themselves and the straight lines which join the principal panels drip with minute foliateness, like lacework, in a style of almost Arabic gorgeousness. The exquisitely carved roof, like the elaborate oak on the Rood Screen, although now white with age, gives a richness to the purple-hued stone of which the fabric itself is composed. A recent discovery by Dean Williams points to the fact that it was the intention of the Norman builders to vault the roof, for at the western end of the Nave above the ceiling have been found the actual baulks of timber let into the structure to carry a raised stone roof. But so beautiful is Treasurer Pole's ceiling, and so distinctive is it in character, that one is led to feel that St. David's is perhaps richer in style for it, than it would have been if the Norman plan had been carried out. The Nave is separated from the aisles by six wide bays, the two westernmost being in Early English style, and the other four Norman. The carving is Early English on Transitional capitals. On the Norman pillars can be seen stone-masons' marks similar to those at Gloucester and Glastonbury. The second Norman pillar in the south aisle bears a fresco of Henry IV, one of the recent discoveries at St. David's. There seems to be no doubt that this fresco and that of the Virgin and the Child on another pillar were temporarily obliterated when the Nave was " beautified " by whitewash during Bishop Field's period (A.D. 1627). Henry's father, John of Gaunt, founded the college of St. Mary—the imposing ruins of which are in the northern portion of the Cathedral Close—in conjunction with Bishop Houghton. Adam Houghton became Lord Chancellor of England under Richard II, and in return for that high appointment he made the King a Prebendary of St. David's. In virtue of this, one of the stalls in the Choir

ST. DAVID'S CATHEDRAL: ST. MARY'S CHAPEL RUINS

ST. DAVID'S CATHEDRAL: ST. DAVID'S ALTAR

belongs to the Sovereign, who holds a cursal prebend. No other British Cathedral has a stall specially set apart for the Ruler of these realms.

Stretching across the Nave is the magnificent stone Choir Screen, built by Henry de Gower (1328–1347), one of the grandest examples of mediæval art in the world. It seems fitting that the famous prelate-architect should have found his last resting-place within the beautiful tomb in the southern recess of the Screen. In the opposite recess are the tombs of unknown priests noteworthy for the canopies, the frescoes of which are remarkably clear. Prior to the restoration of the Cathedral by Sir Gilbert Scott the entrance to the Choir through the Rood Screen was occupied by the tomb of Thomas Bek, Bishop of St. David's (1280–1293), who was also Lord Treasurer, Chancellor of Oxford University, and Keeper of the Great Seal during the absence of Edward I from England in 1279. It was Thomas Bek who defrayed the whole cost of the translation of relics of St. Hugh of Lincoln.

The ritual Choir, occupying the space between the tower and half a bay beyond it, contains some richly carved misereres, erected by Bishop Tully (1460–1481) representing boat-builders, a fox and goose, a knight in a dragon's mouth, four boars killing a dog, and some very fantastically designed serpents and dragons. In the south-western corner is the King's stall. The Bishop's Throne, an elaborate specimen of wood-carving, is the third highest in Great Britain, being exceeded by those in Durham and Exeter Cathedrals. In front of the throne is the grave of John Morgan (the first Welsh Bishop of St. David's since Jorwerth) who constructed the throne partly from materials from Gower's stalls.

In Bishop
Vaughan's Chapel

Another unique feature of the Cathedral is the oak Parclose Screen which here divides the Choir from the Presbytery. This unusual arrangement was undoubtedly designed to prevent pilgrims to the shrine of St. David on the north side of the Presbytery encroaching upon the Choir during divine service. The Lantern has a beautiful Irish oak ceiling glowing with colour and heraldry, including the coats-of-arms of Bishop Tully, Bishop Richard Martin, the friend of Edward IV and Chancellor of Ireland, Treasurer Owen Pole and others who by their gifts or work enriched the Cathedral.

Immediately between the Parclose Screen and the Sanctuary is the rich shrine of Edmund Tudor, father of Henry VII. The four-hundredth anniversary of the day that he was laid to rest beneath the table of massive marble brought from the distant isle of Purbeck is now past: but one can still read the inscription : " Under this Marble Shrine here enclosed resteth the Bones of that noble Lord, Edmund Earl of Richmond, Father and Brother to Kings, the which departed out of this World in the year of our Lord God, a thousand four hundred and fifty and six, the first day of the Month of November; on whose soul Almighty Jesus have mercy. Amen." Tradition declares that Henry VIII refused to grant Bishop Barlow permission to remove the See of St. David's to Carmarthen, because of his respect for the memory of his grandfather whose tomb " had recently been taken from the suppressed priory of Grey Friars at Carmarthen and set up before the High Altar of the Cathedral."

The Presbytery is remarkable for its triforium and clerestory, and pointed arches, with massive stone pillars. The eastern wall contains three large windows, which have been filled in with mosaics by Dr. Salviati of Murano, and four upper lancet windows in substitution for a large Perpendicular fifteenth-century window. The central mosaics depict the Crucifixion, those at the side representing the Church and the Synagogue. The tiling of the sanctuary —before the altar it is Leia's—is very old and very fine. At the back of the High Altar is a pierced window in the form of a cross through which the Altar can be seen from Bishop Vaughan's Chapel.

St. David's Shrine, in the west bay of the north side of the Presbytery, is of the Early English period, built probably by Richard de Carew in 1256. It may be interesting to point out that the old Pilgrims' Door, which gave access to the Shrine through the north transept, has been recently reopened by Dean Williams. The Shrine of St. David's was at one time a great place of pilgrimage. To it came the Conqueror, Henry II, and Edward I with Eleanor, his Queen. It is thought probable that the Canonisation of St. David's, which Henry I brought about in 1131, was due to that monarch's wish to placate the Welsh clergy who had become troublous by Anselm's forceful policy, which resulted in the appointment of Bernard, a Norman monk, to the bishopric in

The Sedilia

1115, thus making St. David's a vassal of Canterbury. Of the pilgrimages to St. David's, one historian says : " Two visits to St. David's tomb were considered equal to one pilgrimage to Rome and three equalled a visit to Jerusalem," an opinion which gave rise to the following hexameter: ROMA SEMEL QUANTUM BIS DAT MENEVIA TANTUM.

On the opposite side of the Presbytery is the exquisite oak sedilia (fifteenth century) and a piscina (twelfth century).

The gem of the Cathedral is undoubtedly Bishop Vaughan's Chapel—the Chapel of the Holy Trinity—between the High Altar and the Lady Chapel. Here in its west wall will be seen the recess of the window at the back of the High Altar formed of five ancient crosses, the bottom one of which is considered to have formed part of the building which preceded Bishop

De Leia's Cathedral. In the recess stands the oaken iron-bound chest containing the bones of St. David and St. Justinian. These relics of the Welsh patron saint and his contemporary were, from some forty years after the canonisation of St. David, contained in a movable shrine. When the Cathedral was restored by Sir Gilbert Scott, the relics were recovered near the High Altar, and were reverently interred in the presence of several people. In 1921 the relics (which had been preserved by the use of liquid cement) were rediscovered during excavations under the direction of Dean Williams, and were placed in the present casket. Since their rediscovery the remains have been examined by prominent surgeons and other experts who are definitely of opinion that the bones are those of a very tall man and a short man. Historical records show that St. David was 6 ft. 4 in. in height, and his contemporary, St. Justinian, was a small man. A portion of a skull undoubtedly reveals that it was that of a man of extraordinary intellect. As Mr. Price (quoted earlier) says : " The Dean's case [that the relics are those of St. David] cannot be ignored." Immediately opposite the chest containing the relics is the Altar, supposed to have been used by St. David between 530 and 601, with five curiously placed crosses, found buried behind the High Altar (where it had been hidden and trodden upon). The base has been built up of very ancient stones, and Celtic crosses. Above St. David's Altar is a fine reredos reconstructed, like the base of the altar, from carvings of the pre-Norman Cathedral. On the left of the Altar is a statue of Bishop Vaughan, and on the right one of Giraldus Cambrensis. The whole chapel, which was in a deplorable condition four years ago, has been renovated in every part at a cost of over £5000, and is now properly fitted and furnished for the due celebration of the Holy Mysteries. Its glory, however, is the finely executed fan-vaulting of the Tudor period.

In St. Thomas's Chapel, now used as the Clergy's Vestry, is the Portable Altar brought by St. David from Jerusalem after his consecration as Bishop by the Patriarch John. The inscription on the Altar is as follows :

> "ALTARE IN QUO SACROSANCTUM MISSÆ SACRIFICIUM CELEBRANDUM EST, DEBET ESSE LAPIDEUM, ET AB EPISCOPO CONSECRATUM : VEL SALTEM ARA LAPIDEA SIMILITER AB EPISCOPO CONSECRATA ET IN EO INSERTA, QUÆ TAM AMPLA SIT, UT HOSTIAM, ET MAJOREM PARTEM CALICIS CAPIAT."

The significance of the Altar in relation to its connection with St. David's Cathedral is considerable, supporting as it does the claim of the independence of the British Church from that of the Church of Rome. The consecration of St. David by John also links up the British Church with Ephesus from where according

The Buttress Arch

to Polycrates in A.D. 196 the Apostle St. John " who lay on the bosom of the Lord " rested and where, according to Irenæus (181–191) St. John lived up to the time of Trajan and published his Gospel. Moreover, within a few years of the consecration of St. David at Jerusalem, the Patriarchate ceased. Another recently discovered relic of St. David is the Font to be seen against the west wall of the Cathedral, a circular column, the top of which is scooped out to form a basin. It speaks much for the zeal and devotion of the Dean and Chapter that the Eastern Chapels (three of which, including the Lady Chapel—restored in 1900 in memory of Bishop Basil Jones, Dean Allen and Dean Owen Phillips— were in utter ruins twenty-five years ago) have been substantially and beautifully restored at a cost of over £10,000. Upon King Edward's Chapel over £3,500 was spent by Viscountess Maidstone, whose desire is to be buried in a tomb there.

Much history of St. David's is contained in the complete roll of Bishops which is to be seen on the western wall of the South Transept. From the time of St. David to that of Novis in 840 there were twenty bishops, including St. Teilo, whose name is linked with that of St. Dubricius of Llandaff. There are the names of Asser (906), the confidant and friend of Alfred the Great ; Samson, described by old Welsh writers as " the Archbishop of the Isle of Britain," and there is also that of Sulien, " the wisest of Britons," received by William the Conqueror.

There is little doubt that until the eleventh century these prelates exercised metropolitan rights and influence not only over South Wales but in districts west of the Severn. According to Mr. H. M. Vaughan " the character and extent of these ancient claims have frequently been made the subject of speculation and controversy among historians, some of whom have not hesitated to designate the early Celtic holders of the See by the title of 'archbishop.' These ill-defined claims were destroyed by St. Anselm's forcible appointment of the Norman monk Bernard. . . ." Those were the days to which Mr. J. A. Price makes allusion, a period which closed with the deprivation of Daniel, the last British Bishop, in 1115. Giraldus Cambrensis (Girald de Barri), the nephew of Bishop Fitzgerald of St. David's, vainly endeavoured to assert that independence and to induce Innocent III to " acknowledge the power of the cathedral chapter to elect its own bishops without reference to English King or primate." Giraldus spent his later years at St. David's, writing his valuable works, where he died in 1223. Other names in the chronological

The Rose Window

96

ST. DAVID'S CATHEDRAL: ST. DAVID'S CASKET

ST. DAVID'S CATHEDRAL: ENTRANCE TO RUINS OF THE BISHOP'S PALACE
(BANQUETING HALL)

Facing page 97

record, besides those already mentioned in this article, are David Martyn (1293), Chancellor of Oxford University; John Thoresby (1347), who became Master of the Rolls, Lord Chancellor and Archbishop of York; John Gilbert (1389), one of the twelve commissioners selected to rule England in the name of Richard II ; Henry Chichele (1408), the Archbishop of Shakespeare's " Henry V " and founder of All Souls, Oxford ; William Barlow (1536), who stripped the lead from the roof of the Cathedral to provide dowries for his five daughters, all of whom married bishops ; Robert Ferrar (1548), burnt at the stake at Carmarthen, and George Bull (1705).

In the wall facing the list of Bishops is a stone cross of considerable antiquarian interest. It is a memorial of great age to Bishop Abraham, who was assassinated by the Danes in 1076. The memorial, in crude lettering, gives the names of Abraham's two sons. The design of this ancient British Cross has been adopted recently for the new Archiepiscopal cross for the Archbishop of Wales. The small Chapter Library in the South Transept contains a number of relics, including croziers, chalices and pattens removed from the tombs of some of the old Bishops during the restoration.

Many of the tombs and monuments in the Cathedral are defaced and mutilated. There are the tombs of Jorwerth, Gower ("Henricus Gower, Episcopalis Palatii Constructor") and other bishops of St. David's, St. Caradoc (1124), Giraldus Cambrensis, Treasurer Thomas Lloyd (1613), a knight and priest (fourteenth century), Sir John Wogan, Chief Justiciary of Ireland under Edward I, the canopied effigies supposed, erroneously it is said, to be those of Prince Rhys (1196) and his son Rhys, and a memorial to the medical staff of the Welsh Hospital in South Africa who died in the Boer War.

Having inspected the Cathedral the visitor will turn to the ruins of the Episcopal Palace on the opposite bank of the Alan. The palace, occupying three sides of a quadrangle 120 feet square, erected by Bishop Gower, must have excelled Lambeth in magnificence. The great banqueting hall, 96 feet by 36 feet, is built over vaulted kitchens and cellars which can still be explored. Intended by Gower for culture and entertainment rather than as a stronghold, the palace was without peer among buildings of its kind and period. In 1633 Bishop Field held a chapter in the Palace.

The ruins of St. Mary's College remain ; and within its precincts has been erected a Retreat House for the clergy. The provision of additional accommodation for the Retreat House and the restoration of the ruins are contemplated, for the completion of which at least £10,000 is required.

The installation of a new heating apparatus and electric machinery during 1925 cost £5,000.

St. David's can be reached by the Great Western Railway motor omnibus services from Mathry-road halt and from Haverfordwest station.

BIRMINGHAM CATHEDRAL

THE Church history of the city of Birmingham is of very recent date. Until the nineteenth century Birmingham was in the Archdeaconry of Coventry, and what little is known in connection with it is to be found in the history of St. Chad's Cathedral of Lichfield. It was not until 1831 that it was felt necessary to transfer Birmingham to the diocese of Worcester. In 1889 Dr. Philpott, then Bishop of Worcester, agreed to give up £600 a year of his income as an endowment for a bishopric of Birmingham ; but it was not until his successor, Bishop Gore, renewed the offer fourteen years later, and added a promise of £10,000, that the scheme was adopted. Within twelve months over £10,500 was collected, and a Bill creating a new See was passed in the following year. Dr. Gore was enthroned as the first Bishop of the See in the Church of St. Philip, Birmingham, in March 1905.

Until the beginning of the eighteenth century there was but one parish church in Birmingham, *i.e.* St. Martin's. As the century opened there appears to have been a revival of Church life, and it was felt that one Church was insufficient to minister to the growing population of the town.

In 1708 an Act of Parliament was passed empowering the Bishop of Coventry and Lichfield to appoint Commissioners to carry out a scheme for a new church to be built. The preamble of the Act is interesting, and after reciting that "whereas the town of Birmingham in the County of Warwickshire being a market town of great trade and commerce has become very populous and hath but one Church in it, which is not sufficient to contain the greater part of the inhabitants, whereby they are deprived of the Divine Service performed there : and the Cemetery of the Church Yard thereof is so little that deceased persons cannot have decent burial," it provides that " for and after the first day of May next ensuing it shall and may be lawful to and for John, Lord Bishop of Coventry and Lichfield, or the Bishop for the time being, to constitute and appoint a certain number of persons by an Instrument in writing under his Episcopal Seal not exceeding the number of 20 to carry out the scheme."

The powers of the Commissioners were to cease within twelve months after the church was erected, built, and finished. It was also indicated that " it shall and may be lawful for Elizabeth Phillips, widow and relict of Robert Phillips, late of Newton Regis in the County of Warwickshire, Esquire ; William Inge of Newton aforesaid, Esquire ; and Elizabeth his wife, and Elizabeth and Penelope, the daughters and co-heirs of the said Robert Phillips, deceased, to convey unto the said supervisors and Commissioners or any five or more of them and their heirs all that Plot or Parcel of Ground with the appertinences in Birmingham aforesaid called or known by the name of the Horse Close, now or late in the tenure or occupation of John Hawkesford."

BIRMINGHAM CATHEDRAL

BIRMINGHAM CATHEDRAL: THE CHOIR

They were also " to provide and set out to the said people as conveniently may be fit a Plot or Parcel of Ground to erect and build a house for the Rector of the said Church, with a back and side Garden and Orchard to the same." The church was for the " use of the inhabitants from time to time inhabiting or to inhabit within that division of the said town called or known by the name of High Town Quarter distinct from other part of the said town." The boundaries of the new parish still survive.

At this time the site of the present Cathedral Church was almost in the country. What is now Colmore Row was known as Newhall Lane, and it formed the southern boundary of the park of the New Hall. This mansion stood almost exactly where the Cathedral House now stands in Newhall Street. Except for the New Hall, there were no houses on the north side of the church, and the district seems to have been practically open country.

The Cathedral Church of St. Philip, Birmingham, was built in 1710 from the design of Thomas Archer, a pupil of Sir John Vanbrugh, and architect of St. John's, Westminster. The building was consecrated four years later, and is very much the same now as then, with the exception of the East end. It cannot be compared with the older Cathedrals, but there is unity in the design. The church stands on the highest point in the city, on the site given by Robert Phillips, and it was as a compliment to him that the church was dedicated to St. Philip.

The original church possessed no Choir, the present one being given by Miss Wilkes as a memorial to her brother. The architect has followed the style of the Nave. The Reredos is of simple design, kept low in order not to interfere with the window above. The altar cross, a beautiful piece of work by Mr. Paul Cooper of the Birmingham School of Art, was given by subscription in 1906.

The most striking features of the church are the windows by Sir Edward Burne-Jones, the glass being by William Morris. The subject of the fine West End window is " The Last Judgment." The upper portion is occupied by a seated figure of Our Lord attended by the Heavenly Host, the centre by an Archangel sounding a trumpet, the background indicating the destruction of all things ; while the lower portion is filled with a dignified group of wondering mortals raised from their long sleep within the tombs in which they stand. The effect is remarkably dramatic, and should be seen at sunset, when the colours are truly magnificent. The subjects of the Eastern windows are the Nativity, the Ascension, and the Crucifixion. Worth noting are the iron gates, which are similar to those in St. Paul's Cathedral. Above the south-west door is the following : " His Most Excellent Majesty, King George, upon the kind application of Sir Richard Gough to the Right Honourable Sir Robert Walpole, gave £600 towards furnishing this church, A.D. 1725."

In the vestry, on the south side of the Choir, the registers, dating from 1714, and the original contracts for the building of the church, are preserved, with the minutes of the vestry meetings, which are interesting and give a good idea of the character of eighteenth-century Church administration in Birmingham. One entry made in 1715 reads : " Ordered (to avoid all disturbance in ye Church) y^t every person shall take their place in their seat as they come, and not to strive for any particular place. Ordered, y^t if it shall happen there should be any dispute between any persons about taking any place in ye seat, ye person who subscribes most to ye said Church shall be preferred."

American visitors will note particularly the Maryland flag presented to the present Rector, Bishop Hamilton Baynes, on his mission to Maryland in 1922. The connection between Maryland and the Church of England in this diocese is interesting. A Dr. Bray, born in 1656, was in the year 1690 appointed rector of Sheldon, just outside Birmingham, the patron of the living being Lord Digby, who was one of the builders of the Cathedral Church. In 1695–96 Dr. Bray was appointed by Bishop Compton, the then Bishop of London, to proceed to Maryland to assist the Church there in its weakness. To help him in his work he founded the S.P.C.K. in 1698. Dr. Bray sailed for Maryland in 1699, and the following year he returned to England to report that, in his opinion, another missionary society was needed in order to supply the living agents for these distant plantations. This was the S.P.G. He petitioned the King and Queen (William and Mary), who proved to be sympathetic with the movement, and a charter for the proposed new society was read at a Committee of the S.P.C.K. on May 3, 1701, and signed and sealed on June 16. It will thus be evident that it was an important service which Dr. Bray, the Sheldon rector, rendered to the English people throughout the world by calling into being two great societies—namely, the Society for Promoting Christian Knowledge and the Society for the Propagation of the Gospel, which have for over 200 years been working side by side.

The Maryland flag hanging in Birmingham Cathedral recalls a portion of American history. The first permanent British settlement in America was in Virginia in 1607. In 1624 James I deprived the Virginia Company of their Charter, and in 1632 Charles I gave to Sir Charles Calvert absolute proprietary rights of the whole of Maryland and Delaware, and parts of Pennsylvania and Virginia, which province Sir Charles called Maryland, in honour of the Queen Henrietta Maria. The Calvert arms, which with those of the Crossland family appear on the flag, are, in heraldic language, " Paly of six or, on sable, a bend counter-changed." Those of the Crossland family are, " Quarterly argent and gules, a cross botonny counter-changed." This flag has remained, ever since, the flag of Maryland, and is the oldest in America.

There is nothing noteworthy about the structural part of the exterior of the Cathedral. The Tower, which has a rugged appearance and stands out from the rest of the building, contains a fine peal of ten bells.

CHESTER CATHEDRAL

CHESTER CATHEDRAL: THE CHOIR

CHESTER CATHEDRAL

IN Roman times the City of the Marches was Deva, and the best example in Britain of a purely military fortress. As Bishop Mandell Creighton wrote—This was the Castrum *par excellence*. It was the great station of the XXth Legion (*Valeria Victrix*), whose badge was the charging boar, still so familiar a sight in Chester. During the five centuries which followed the departure of the Romans, *circa* 410, Chester passed through troublous times until Ethelfleda, "the Lady of the Mercians," made extensive repairs and additions to the fortifications of the city. Ethelfleda was responsible also for the erection of a church, upon the site of which St. Peter's now stands.

Chester—the last city in England to hold out for Harold—from Norman times became an important ecclesiastical centre, with foundations for the Benedictine, Dominican, and other monastic orders. The Benedictine order was represented by the Abbey of St. Werburgh, built upon the site of an old Saxon church, claimed by the monks to have been erected " soon after Lucius and afore King Arthure," dedicated to St. Peter and St. Paul. " I find no mention of a bishop at Chester," says Leycester in his *Prolegomena*, " before the Norman Conquest, only we read that Dwina, a Scotchman, was made bishop of Mercia by King Oswy, whereof Cheshire was a small parcel." Heylin gives a list of thirty-four bishops, beginning with Dwina and ending with Peter, A.D. 1067. " Hoveden," to quote Leycester again, " says that Chester was a bishop's see whilst it was under the dominion of the Britons." A traditional version is that, connected with the Saxon church at Chester, was a nunnery which Ethelfleda replaced by a College of Secular Canons. To this church, in 874, was brought the body of St. Werburgh from Hanbury in Staffordshire, to save it from the Danes and to do more honour to her memory, and at that time the dedication was changed to her name. Of St. Werburgh, the daughter of Wulfere, King of Mercia, it is told that she was the humblest, and most obedient, and the most given to prayer of all that monarch's saintly family. Though many great nobles would fain have married her, she would have none of them. She said, " I am wedded to Christ and His Church." This caused her much trouble, for her lovers and relations were wroth with her. At last she was allowed to enter the great Abbey of Ely, where her aunt, St. Etheldreda, ruled as abbess. Here her life was so exact that her uncle, King Ethelred, made her supervisor of all the nunneries in his realm, and these she brought to a perfect state of observance, by her own life inciting others to follow more closely in the steps of Christ. She died at Trentham A.D. 699, and was buried at Hanbury. Ethelfleda's college was further endowed by King Edgar, and later was again extended by the great Earl Leofric, the husband of Lady Godiva. The change from the College of Secular Canons was made in 1093 by Hugh

Lupus, the first Norman Earl of Chester, and a nephew of the Conqueror. The Welshmen of that day called him "Hugh Vras," *i.e.* Hugh the Fat. Leycester cites Ordericus as calling him "Hugh Dirgane, that signifies in the Welsh language Hugh the Gross : for he was very gross and corpulent."*

Pulpit in Refectory

"Anselm came to England," says Trevisa in his translation of Higden's *Polychronicon*, "at the entreaty of Hugh, Earl of Chester, then sick ; by whose help the Earl founded a monastery at Chester wherein Anselm placed Richard his Chaplain, the first Abbot, and turned the secular canons into regular monks."

While this monastery was being erected Peter, the first Norman Bishop of Mercia, built the Church of St. John the Baptist—a fine Norman edifice, still in existence, on the other side of the Walls. Peter had moved his seat from Lichfield to Chester in 1075, where it remained until 1102, when Coventry was chosen. It was still the same diocese and was sometimes referred to as the diocese of Lichfield, Coventry and Chester. Throughout the Middle Ages the Bishops of Lichfield were often called Bishops of Coventry. Giraldus and the Archbisop Baldwin (who had been preaching the Crusade through Wales) were at Chester on St. John's Day, 1187, and it appears from the itinerary that they received cheese of deer's milk from the Countess of Chester and her mother.

"The history of the Abbey," according to the excellent little "Handbook for Pilgrims to Chester Cathedral," "is a series of quarrels between powerful Abbots and the Nobles, and, later on, the citizens. We are left to imagine the quieter and much more important life of the community itself—the scholars working at their books, the artists at their illuminations, the gardeners at their flowers and vegetables. We cannot doubt that St. Werburgh's was great in its hospitality, generous to the poor, and a teacher to the young. Here at least, amid all the strife and bloodshed of those rough times, the praises of GOD never ceased in surroundings of a kind that only the mediæval Church could produce."

In 1541, at the Dissolution of the Monasteries, Henry VIII converted the Abbey into the Cathedral Church of the new Diocese of Chester, to be served by a dean and six canons. The last Abbot, Thomas Clark, became the first Dean of the new foundation, and so the continuity of the services remained unbroken. At this time the dedication was changed to that of CHRIST AND THE BLESSED VIRGIN. While, as a distinct See, Chester is not earlier than Henry VIII's time, yet the Cathedral possesses remains of a Norman architecture, giving it a special interest, and it is even possible to enable the imagination to reproduce not only the form and dimensions but the very appearance of the old Norman edifice with tolerable accuracy, notwithstanding the existing

* Ormerod's " History of Cheshire."

CHESTER CATHEDRAL: THE CLOISTERS

CHESTER CATHEDRAL: THE REFECTORY

preponderance of Decorated and Perpendicular work. As Dr. W. R. Lethaby, the surveyor of Westminster Abbey, has written : " These stones were wrought by our forefathers in the land from time to time during all the centuries of British history onward from the Norman Conquest. Knowledge that we have such a past and actual contact with it in our great monuments should be strengthening and rest-giving to all who will think of it."

Parts of Anselm's Norman church are to be seen in the North Nave wall and in the basement of the North-western Tower. This basement is now used as a Baptistery, containing a Venetian font, probably sixth-century work— presented by the late Earl of Egerton—which forms the oldest possession of the Cathedral, and above which hangs a Jacobean lantern. The North Transept, though raised in height, remains of the size designed by Anselm, and retains much very early work. The arcading of the eastern wall is the work of early artificers. On a boss in the roof are the arms of Cardinal Wolsey, which are repeated in the Cloisters. The position of the arch of the original Apse is still apparent, but probably the existence of the domestic dwellings of the monks prevented the extension of the Transept.

The fact that the South Transept is much larger than the North is thought to be due to the growth of the monastery and the need for more chapels and altars. To extend the Transept the parishioners of St. Oswald's Church were ejected, another church being built for them in another part of the city. Later, however, there was considerable quarrelling between the monks and the parishioners, the latter having demanded the return of their old church. Eventually the monks gave way, and until 1880 the Transept was a separate church apart from the Cathedral. Quite recently the Transept has been restored as a memorial to Hugh Lupus, first Duke of Westminster, and a great benefactor to the Cathedral. It has fine Decorated and Perpendicular windows and wooden vaulting.

The Nave is the work of a very long period, stretching from Abbot Richard de Seynesbury (1349–63) to the work of Abbot Birchenshaw (1493–1537) at the western end, shortly before the Dissolution. It was a period of great quarrels with the citizens. The work was often broken off for the want of money, and because the monks were more set on upholding the honour of their house than on building. Consequently, the Nave is of very broken design, and even the North and South Clerestories are substantially different. Further, by the middle of the fifteenth century the shrine of St. Werburgh had lost some of its popularity, and the number of pilgrims to the shrine with their offerings diminished. The work therefore has little ornament, and the Triforium and Clerestory are run into one. Sir Gilbert Scott's wooden vaulting has undoubtedly

Miserere : The Story of St. Werburgh

increased the dignity of the Nave, which before had a flat wooden roof. Among the finest features are the capitals of the pillars, one of which bears the initials of Abbot Simon Ripley (1485–93), during whose seven years' rule there was peace, and the work bearing his mark is finer than the rest. The Nave originally ended one bay west of the Central Tower, where a stone screen cut it off from the Choir. There is an entirely different design in this eastern bay of the Nave. "Above here," says the Cathedral Handbook, " by the Clerestory window can be seen the little chained man the monks put to frighten away the devil, when he came to pry at them in choir over the screen." The panels behind the nave choir stalls are of great beauty. Over the Choir entrance is the Rood, an immense addition to the glory of the Cathedral, placed there by Dean Darby. The carving was done in the Austrian Tyrol.

The Lady Chapel is a fine specimen of Early English work on the part of Abbot Simon Whitchurch (1265–90). At the west end stands the restored shrine of St. Werburgh, around the top of which are forty figures of the royal line of Mercia. For years the base of this shrine formed part of the Bishop's throne. The high altar is constructed from various woods from Palestine, oak from Bashan, cedar from Lebanon, and olive from the Mount of Olives.

The Choir, which is 125 feet long, is transitional Early English Decorated, containing a series of carved stalls of the late fourteenth-century period which are the chief glory of the Cathedral. Many of the carvings are unsurpassed in England, and their quaint symbols will be carefully studied by the visitor. The bench-ends to the Dean's and Sub-Dean's stall are evidences of highly skilled workmanship. The triforium arcade is also specially notable. Near the vestry is a small fireplace used by the monks to bake the eucharistic bread and heat the charcoal for incense.

The Cathedral has a number of interesting chapels. In one on the south side is the flag in which the body of General Wolfe was wrapped after his death on the Heights of Abraham. At the junction of the Transept and Nave near a large niche is the flag of H.M.S. *Chester*, with the ship's own Roll of Honour. This flag was flying through the battle of Jutland, and under it Jack Cornwell gained the Victoria Cross. In the stone bench along the wall of the south choir aisle is the tomb of one of the greatest of the Chester Cathedral community, Ralph Higden, a brother of the Monastery, and author of the great mediæval history of the world, the *Polychronicon* already referred to. He is also a possible author of the Chester cycle of miracle plays which were acted throughout the city by the various trade guilds in Whitsun Week. These plays represented the more important Scripture stories and were of enormous interest and value, both for their presentation of the Bible in a form which appealed particularly to the unlettered folk of the Middle Ages, and for the place which they occupy in the development of the English stage.

The conventual buildings will attract the attention of the visitor. The domestic buildings are undergoing restoration, with the laudable object in view of making these play once again an important part in the life of the Diocese. It is the hope of the Dean and Chapter to utilise these buildings in the near future for a number of diocesan purposes—meetings, quiet days, religious plays, conferences, and for catering for pilgrims to the Cathedral. These restorations are bringing to light again much of the old-time beauty of the Monastery. At the east end of the South Cloister is a particularly fine Norman door. Undoubtedly this cloister was the chief working-place of the monks, and principally of those engaged in copying sacred writings. The great cellar of the Abbey, a fine Norman Undercroft, is to be seen on the west side of the West Cloister. The North Cloister occupies the whole length of the Refectory, built by Simon de Whitchurch. Whitchurch was the abbot who gave great assistance to Edward I in his conflicts with the Welsh. The Refectory is Early English, with Perpendicular windows, and is largely as it was left by Whitchurch (1265–90). There is here the exquisite Early English lector's pulpit, from which a lection is still read when the Great Chapter, or the officers of the Cathedral, breakfast or dine in the Refectory. When restored the Refectory will closely resemble the famous halls of our ancient Universities. The Chapter House vestibule in the East Cloister, which is considered to be one of the finest of the ecclesiastical buildings, may also have been the work of Abbot Simon.

The Chapter House itself, with its lancet windows and their great detached shafts, is a splendid example of late thirteenth-century work. This was the business room of the Abbey, where also the confessions of the monks were heard. Chapter and other meetings are now held in this room, and here the Great Chapter, composed of both honorary and residentiary canons, comes together, under the presidency of the Bishop. At the east end is the Cathedral Sacristy, containing an old cupboard, with wooden doors hewn and smoothed by axe, and overlaid with particularly beautiful hand-wrought iron work of the thirteenth century. It has been restored to what was its original use, the Cathedral's Cope Chest. Near by in another old cupboard are kept the chasubles and other vestments.

The visitor should not omit to inspect the Norman Chapel of St. Anselm, the Abbot's Chapel now used by Chester's Bishops. The whole of the Cathedral, with its nine furnished chapels and the old domestic buildings of the Monastery, including the Refectory, the Parlour, and the great Undercroft, are open, without fee of any kind, from 7.30 A.M. to dark every day, including Sundays. A " Little Handbook for Pilgrims " is provided, so that visitors can be their own guides and enjoy one of the most interesting and beautiful of the mediæval churches of England at their own leisure. To this interesting Handbook (price 3d.) the compiler of this account of the Cathedral is considerably indebted, by kind permission of the author, Mr. F. L. M. Bennett.

MANCHESTER CATHEDRAL

THE Cathedral Church of Manchester, dedicated to "the Glorious Virgin, and the Holy Martyrs, St. Denys and St. George," stands on the site of a Saxon church built when much of the present busy and important part of the Cotton-opolis was the moated grounds of a thegn's hall bounded on the west and north by the rivers Irwell and Irk. When the restoration of the Cathedral was in progress in 1882, certain stones were discovered which were considered to point to the existence of this Saxon edifice until the thirteenth century, when a substantial Early English church was created to which additions were made in the fourteenth century. That an ecclesiastical establishment existed at Manchester in the reign of Edward the Confessor is evident from the Domesday Book, but as regards the original church or any succeeding buildings on the site very little is known prior to the year 1422. A valuable relic known as the Angel Stone, bearing an inscription of Saxon date, is preserved in the Consistory Court. In 1421 Thomas, Lord de la Warre, who since 1373 had been Rector of Manchester, received licence from Henry V to collegiate the church, which was the first and only Collegiate church in the county. Giving his baronial hall as a residence for the Collegiates, De la Warre appointed as first master or warden John Huntingdon, who built a new Choir ; the Nave being subsequently rebuilt, mainly on the lines of Early English Nave, by Ralph Langley, fourth Warden. Huntingdon's fine memorial brass (restored) is in the Choir.

The sixth Warden, James Stanley, who afterwards became the Bishop of Ely, was responsible for much of the fine work in the present Cathedral. He greatly changed Huntingdon's Choir, moving the north arcade to provide for the beautiful choir stalls with which his name and that of Mr. Beswick or Bexwicke, a Manchester merchant, are connected.

To Stanley was due also the octagonal Chapter House, the present form of the Clerestories and roofs of the Nave and Choir, and the fine Choir screen and east window. He was also co-founder with Sir John Stanley, Kt., of the large chapel of St. John the Baptist on the north side of the Choir, now known as the Derby Chapel, adjoining which is the Ely Chapel where the remains of the Bishop found their last resting place. The tomb is modern, but it retains portions of the ancient brasses and inscription.

The exterior of the Cathedral, originally built of local red sandstone, was refaced with more durable gritstone in the latter half of the nineteenth century, the Tower being completely rebuilt and several extensions, including the three porches, added. An extensive renewal of the interior of the Nave was also carried out, the only original stonework in this part of the church being the arch leading into the Tower which contains panelling (much defaced) affording evidence of the widening of the church during Stanley's period of office.

MANCHESTER CATHEDRAL: THE NAVE

MANCHESTER CATHEDRAL: THE NAVE, LOOKING NORTH-EAST FROM THE
SOUTH DOOR AND SHOWING VISTA OF PILLARS

Facing page 107

The outstanding feature of the interior of the Cathedral is its unusual width, the outer aisles of the Nave occupying the sites of four chantry chapels, thus giving an extreme measurement of 115 feet, and affording an example of arcaded work such as is rarely met with.

The chief glory of the Cathedral, however, is its woodwork, which embraces as many as seventeen screens and a range of choir stalls of supreme and in some respects unique excellence, of the screens those of the Lady Chapel (*circa* 1440), Jesus Chapel (1506), and the great quire screen (restored) are particularly fine specimens.

The Choir stalls are notable not only for their elaborate carving, but also as presenting three examples of canopy design and possessing a unique tester or cornice which surmounts the canopies. The design belongs to the latest period of the fifteenth century, although the work was probably not completed until slightly later, when the northern stalls were added, being the gift of Richard Beswicke, whose cipher appears on the shield at the east end. On the stall desk of the Canons-in-Residence are carved the arms of De La Warre, the founder of the College; whilst in the Dean's stall the story of the child of the Lathom family carried off by an eagle is portrayed, underneath being the arms of Thomas Stanley, Earl of Derby, father of the Warden, who died in 1504.

It is from the entrance to the Derby Chapel that the visitor to the Cathedral will gather a fine conception of the pillared work of the Nave, although entrance by the South Porch will probably give a more lasting impression of the glorious vista for which the church is noted. Each of the principals of the Nave roof is supported by carved figures of angels, with "instruments of musick"—wind on the north side and stringed on the south side—

of that rare character which marks the famous Minstrels' Gallery of Exeter Cathedral. It is said, however, that the clavicymbal on the north side,

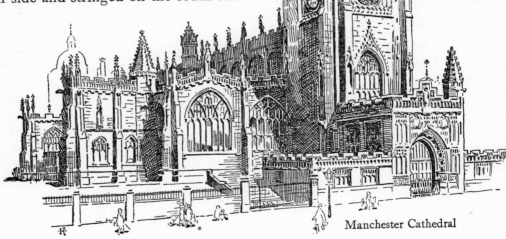

Manchester Cathedral

transferred by mistake from the south side at the last restoration, is the only existing representation of an angel playing this particular instrument.

The history of the Collegiate Church shows that the college suppressed in the reign of Edward VI was restored by charter by Queen Mary and remodelled by an Elizabethan Charter. The Charter by which it is at present governed was granted by Charles I styling it " The College of Christ in Manchester, founded by King Charles." By Act of Parliament of 1840, however, which changed certain official titles in Cathedral and Collegiate Churches, the Wardens and Fellows became styled Dean and Canons of the Collegiate Church, and by order in Council power was given to Manchester preserving all the privileges and exemptions connected with its foundation. Seven years later, on the constitution of the Bishopric of Manchester, the Collegiate Church became the Cathedral Church of the new Diocese, and practically, with the exceptions before named, the interior stands mainly as the fine craftsmen of the fifteenth century left it. Like Westminster Abbey and certain other great religious foundations, the exterior has suffered considerably by the chemical properties air-borne from the chimneys of great factories, which has rendered necessary the replacing of the original soft stone by more durable material.

Of the great part which Manchester Cathedral plays as the centre of the religious life of the great industrial centre there can be no possible doubt. It is, indeed, deeply rooted. " It may be confidently asserted," wrote the late Dean of Manchester (the Very Rev. J. Gough McCormick), " that no Cathedral holds a higher place in the hearts of the people among whom it stands than does that of Manchester. ' T'owd church,' as it is often affectionately called, has a very real influence, broad and deep, upon the life, secular as well as religious, of our great city."

LIVERPOOL CATHEDRAL

LIVERPOOL CATHEDRAL : CHOIR LOOKING EAST

LIVERPOOL CATHEDRAL

TWENTY-ONE years have wellnigh elapsed since the late King Edward laid the foundation-stone of Liverpool Cathedral. Its completion—a work of years yet—will mark the third cathedral of the Established Church erected since the Dissolution : first, St. Paul's Cathedral, entirely rebuilt after the Great Fire of London ; Truro ; and now Liverpool. Another great cathedral built since then is Bentley's Westminster Cathedral, the seat of the Cardinal Archbishop of the Roman Catholic Church in this country.

The aim of the Liverpool Cathedral Building Committee is inspiring. The success of their efforts will mean that Liverpool Cathedral will take its place among the largest ecclesiastical edifices in the world—St. Peter's, Rome, Seville, Cordova, and Milan Cathedrals. In length Liverpool Cathedral will be some fifty feet longer than Old St. Paul's, and will exceed in area York Minster by more than one-half. When completed Liverpool Cathedral will be more than double the size of Westminster Abbey. Of the date of the completion of this great building it is impossible to speak, but, compared with the duration of building operations by the Great Masters of the Norman Period, the work is proceeding steadily and with no undue delay ; the same idea permeates these twentieth-century builders—the building is not for to-day only but for posterity. It will assuredly be a fine monument to the religious ideals of the great industrial and commercial population of the city and of the palatinate and the nation as a whole. No better site could have been chosen for such a monument than St. James's Mount—an uplifted rocky mass in the centre of the city, 155 feet above the Mersey.

The Diocese of Liverpool was established in 1880, St. Peter's Parish Church being assigned as the Cathedral, with Dr. John Charles Ryle as the first Bishop. The proposal to erect a new Cathedral took tangible form seven years later, and at the Diocesan Conference of 1900, Dr. Ryle's successor, Bishop Chavasse, who has now been succeeded, after a 23 years' episcopate, by the Rt. Rev. A. A. David, enunciated a bold policy for a Cathedral worthy of and suited to the requirements of the city. " In the Cathedral of which I dream," said the Bishop, " there would be daily services of the best and most reverent kind for the rich and the poor, at hours suited to both. There would be smaller chapels where Quiet Days for clergy and laity would be held, and where lectures on Church questions would be delivered. Attached to it would be a staff of Cathedral clergy, not holding other benefices, but living and working entirely for the diocese. There would be Canons to whom would be entrusted, as at Exeter, the oversight of religious education, the management of parochial missions, the supervision of junior clergy, the fostering of an interest in the spread of the Gospel at home and abroad. There

109

would be clergy able to look after vacant parishes, and to go to the help of sick vicars. There would be others, with special gifts for preaching, who would assist the clergy by taking courses of sermons in Lent and Advent, and by lecturing throughout the diocese on Christian Evidences, Biblical Criticism, Church History, and the Best Methods of Church Work. There would be something like a central school of Church music, which, while seeking to make our singing more congregational than it is at present, would set the tone of a high-class and devotional service."

So high an ideal, presented in so hopeful a way, kindled much earnest enthusiasm, and matters rapidly progressed.

The site of St. James's Mount having been selected, the Advisory Architects, Messrs. R. G. Bodley, R.A., and R. Norman Shaw, R.A., selected the plans of Mr. Giles Gilbert Scott (now Sir Giles Gilbert Scott, R.A.), then barely twenty-one years of age. Mr. G. F. Bodley and Mr. Gilbert Scott acted as joint architects, but since the death of Mr. Bodley, in 1907, Mr. Scott has been responsible for the work. Mr. Scott, the grandson of Sir Gilbert Scott, whose name will long be associated with the nineteenth-century revival of ecclesiastical architecture in Great Britain, has designed a truly noble structure. The Central Tower, 342 feet in height, will dominate the city and the Mersey, and will be a landmark from the Dee estuary and the sea. Mr. Scott's work has been described as a free interpretation of fourteenth-century Gothic, possessing classic simplicity and symmetry of design. As a recent writer said, " In considering the Gothic design alone it is remarkable how far Mr. Scott has travelled from the purely imitative Gothic of his grandfather's many mid-Victorian churches. In a single building he is perhaps doing more than any other architect to combat the idea that the Gothic spirit is dead, and that buildings built to-day in the Gothic style can be nothing more than a repetition of that of which the living spirit cannot be recaptured."

The Cathedral will seat 7000 people, while the Choir and Transepts will give accommodation for about 1200 worshippers in addition to clergy and choristers. The vaulting of the Nave and Choir will be higher than that of any other English cathedral. The narrowness of the site has led to a happy reversion to an old ecclesiastical custom. The greatest length of the site is from north-west to south-east, and for this reason the " east " end of Liverpool Cathedral will be almost due south. This, it is pointed out, in the Official Handbook published by the Cathedral Committee, is correct according to old ecclesiastical usage, since the ancient custom was to plan the church, not due east and west, but so that the window over the high altar should look to the part of the horizon where the sun rises on the feast day of the saint in whose name the church was dedicated. The Cathedral is to be called " The Cathedral Church of Christ," and on Christmas Day the sun rises at that part of the heavens to which the great window over the Holy Table looks.

This great window forms one of the most prominent features of the great edifice. From the sill, 46 feet above the floor level, the window rises 76 feet

LIVERPOOL

BIRMINGHAM

OXFORD

CHESTER

MANCHESTER

by 44 feet wide, with a large circular window at the apex. The stained glass tells of the "Te Deum."

The Cathedral is to consist of a Choir of three bays, 152 feet long, and adjoining Transepts each 52 feet long and the same in width (forming the first portion to be completed and consecrated), leading to a wide central space 190 feet by 87 feet, over which will be a Tower 342 feet high. On the other side of the centre the design is symmetrically repeated, with a second pair of Transepts and a Nave of three bays. The height of

Detail of Organ Gallery

the Choir is 116 feet, and its width 47 feet, or, including the aisles, 87 feet. The width of the arch of the central space is 63 feet. The total exterior length of the building as planned, including the Lady Chapel, is 611 feet. The subjects of the beautiful Reredos are the Crucifixion, the Lord's Supper, and other details of the Passion. Sixty-five feet in height, and of red sandstone, it occupies the whole width of the Sacrarium.

In the Choir aisles are three windows, each of two lights, in each aisle. At the East end the aisles have a low barrel vault, carrying a floor above, and each is lighted by a rose window in the East wall. At the West end the vault is similar. Here will be placed the Organ, which occupies the western bays on both sides of the Choir, and the two windows of these bays, being obscured by it, will not be available for lighting. The remaining windows, two on each side, have been filled with stained glass. Behind and outside the main East wall is the Ambulatory, connecting the two Choir aisles, and lighted by four two-light windows. At the North end of the Ambulatory lies the Chapter House, the gift of the Freemasons of the Province of West Lancashire, and at the South the Lady Chapel. Between the bays and overlooking the Choir, the Triforium has carved tracery screens extending from pier to pier of the arcades ; and each bay is covered with a barrel vault, divided into panels by ribs. The four great transverse arches spanning the Choir are fully moulded.

The North-east Transept will be set apart as a Memorial Chapel in memory of those sailors and soldiers in the Great War, who were born in the Diocese of Liverpool and the Wirral, or whose families were resident there. It is Liverpool's monument to her sons who gave their lives in the Great War. At the East end of the North and South aisles will stand two small towers connected with a walking way above the great window. The entrance to the Lady Chapel, known as the Children's Porch, has been provided by gifts from the children and young people of the Diocese.

Since 1910 services have been held in the fine Lady Chapel, whose connection with Liverpool goes back to the seventeenth century. The Chapel is remarkable for its strength, grace, and simplicity, and is the keynote to Mr. Scott's great work. The internal size of the Chapel is 120 feet long by 33 feet 6 inches wide, including the aisles, the width between the arcade walls being 25 feet. It is divided into six bays and finished in a three-sided apse. It is two-storied, a narrow gallery running along the bottom of the clerestory, protected by a stone screen and finished with a deep cresting of roses, thistles, shamrocks, and lilies, with projecting figures of angels and minstrels. The windows of the apse have three lights, and the tracery is of great beauty. All the windows are filled with stained glass. The Mother and Child, with the Magi, fill the centre window ; holy women of the Old and New Testaments, with the Annunciation and Presentation, are to the north and south ; and in the other windows are figures of holy women of olden time. The stem of the Tree of Life is shown in the centre light, and its branches are seen in all the windows. The general effect is extremely rich, and the details are delightful. The stone vault, the effect of which is admirable, is a barrel (with ribs and bosses) cut for the windows ; and along the ridge the ribs form traceried panels. Above it is an ample chamber, covered with a roof of oak and copper. The West end is very effective. Over the narthex or ante-chapel lies a wide-spreading arch ; above this three arches of a stone gallery carry the organ loft, with its chaste front of carved oak and two stone guardian angels, one at each end, and the exquisite woodwork of the organ-case reaching up into the vault.

The foundation-stone of the Cathedral was laid on July 19th, 1904, by King Edward VII, who was accompanied by Queen Alexandra ; and King George V and Queen Mary were present at the consecration of the Choir on July 19, 1924. During the evening following the consecration King George knighted Mr. Gilbert Scott in recognition of his work for Liverpool's Cathedral.

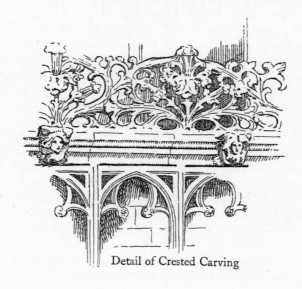

Detail of Crested Carving

TO THE READER

THE chapters of this volume have been arranged in an order which it is felt will coincide with the plans of most of our visitors from Overseas who may be contemplating a tour of the principal Cathedral cities of England and Wales. The book deals specifically with Westminster and Bath Abbeys and the twenty Anglican Cathedrals within the area served by the Great Western Railway—churches which will be found to contain most of the outstanding architectural features of the famous Cathedrals of Great Britain. In the chapter on Bristol Cathedral space has been devoted to St. Mary Redcliffe, the celebrated church in that city, remarkable for its architecture and for its associations.

The section dealing with Cathedral Architecture will enable many of the visitors to understand the various styles and periods of buildings.

The reader is presumed to be making London the starting-point for such a tour, and for this reason the opening chapters deal with Westminster Abbey, St. Paul's Cathedral, and St. Saviour's Cathedral, Southwark.

The grouping of the Cathedrals has also been arranged in an order which it is felt will be found suitable by readers who may desire to give more leisure to their inspection of these famous churches. Any readers desiring information as to train services to the various cities, and other information concerning Great Western Railway facilities, are requested to write to the Superintendent of the Line, Great Western Railway, Paddington, W.

Space has not permitted an elaborate and detailed treatment of these wonderful churches, replete with the work of great master builders ; but an attempt has been made to present much of outstanding interest. Among the pictorial illustrations will be found photographic reproductions which are unique, and care has been taken to record by black-and-white drawings some of the proudest possessions of these Cathedrals. The compiler of this book desires to express his appreciation of the help he has received from the Cathedral authorities, and for the facilities given to obtain illustrations.

G. E. B.

Pipe and Tabor on a Misericord, Exeter Cathedral

CATHEDRALS

And how to understand their Architecture *[By Martin S. Briggs, F.R.I.B.A.]* Being a Supplementary Section to CATHEDRALS (published by the *G.W.R.*, London, Eng.)

SCOTLAND

NORTH SEA

IRISH SEA

Liverpool
Manchester
Chester

WALES

Birmingham
Worcester
Hereford

Saint Davids

Brecon
Gloucester
St. Woolos (Newport)
G.W.R.
Oxford
Llandaff

BRISTOL CHANNEL

Bristol Bath G.W.R. LONDON

Wells

Salisbury Winchester

Exeter

Truro

ENGLISH CHANNEL

M.S.B.

GLOUCESTER

WINCHESTER

OXFORD

NORMAN (*c.* 1066–*c.* 1160)

ALTHOUGH the cathedrals and abbeys described in this volume contain several fragments of Saxon work, the first style of which noteworthy examples remain is " Norman," or, more correctly, " English Romanesque " architecture, i.e. the English equivalent of the Romanesque style that arose in Western Europe as it recovered from the Dark Ages that followed the fall of Roman civilisation. Romanesque architecture, in England as on the Continent, is derived and developed from the Roman fashion of building with massive arches that may be seen in the great aqueducts and amphitheatres. The use of columns, too, structural as well as decorative, was adopted from Rome, where they had been employed as explained in the last paragraph of this book. The type of building on which Romanesque architecture was based was the late Roman basilica, with a nave and aisles. But it was a distinct and vigorous style, varying considerably in the different countries where it grew up, yet possessing many characteristics common to all its forms. There was Romanesque building in France before the eleventh century, but when Duke William invaded this country his own duchy of Normandy had not advanced very far in developing the new style. The Conquest was followed by great building activity, radiating northwards and westwards from London, so that it reached the western counties last of all. Church-building was largely in the hands of the religious orders, thus the Benedictines founded Winchester, Chester, and Gloucester cathedrals as monastic churches.

Norman architecture is characterised by its massiveness, by round arches, by relatively small windows, by heavy vaulting, and by simple " cushion " capitals cut out of a solid cube of stone (*see sketch*). Piers were sometimes plain cylinders, as at Gloucester (*see sketch*), but more often moulded. Ornamental features, except for occasional grotesque heads, etc., are of a stiff and geometrical type, chief among them being the zig-zag or chevron pattern that may be seen round the doorway from Oxford (*see sketch*).

EXAMPLES: Winchester, 1079–93 (the nave and choir being Norman work now concealed by later casing) ; Hereford choir, 1079–1110, and nave, 1131–48 ; Gloucester, 1089–1120 (mostly cased like Winchester in later years) ; Chester north transept, 1093 ; Llandaff choir, 1120–33 ; Exeter towers, 1112–36 ; Bristol chapter-house and gateways, 1150–70 ; Oxford, 1154–80 ; and St. David's, begun 1180.

EARLY ENGLISH (*c*.1200–*c*.1250)

BETWEEN 1160 and 1200 English architecture began to develop rapidly into a native style, as the skill of English masons allowed them to dispense with their French teachers. Thus we find the round arch surviving at St. David's (*c*. 1180), but even there changes were appearing, and in many other places the round arch had by that time given place to the pointed arch, which was, in one form or another, the most characteristic feature of the Gothic styles that prevailed in this country till the middle of the sixteenth century. The influence of the Cistercian monks from Burgundy was at its greatest during this period. The invention of the pointed arch is now generally attributed to the Saracens, and first appears in the mosque of Ibn Tulun (868–79) in Cairo, but as to this there is still a difference of opinion. Its importance in architectural development is structural rather than decorative, for it enabled the builders to cover large churches with stone vaulted roofs, and so to avoid the risk of fire that was always present in such Norman churches as were covered with wooden roofs only. The stone vaults used by the Normans were of such a form that their immense weight put a great strain on the walls and piers that carried them. In this short sketch it is impossible to treat of vaulting, but it must be remembered that the whole story of Gothic architecture is really the story of vaulting. For four hundred years the builders were striving to reduce the piers and walls that carried the vaulted roof, and then to increase the size of the windows as the use of stained glass became general in later years, till at last we find such examples as the chapel of Henry the Seventh at Westminster (1500–12), where the richly ornamented roof of stone vaulting rises from slender piers of stone that barely interrupt a wall-surface which is practically a screen of stained glass. But, because the question of vaulting is so complex, a casual visitor to our cathedrals will find it convenient to differentiate the styles by equally distinctive though less vital features, and it is with such that this brief outline is concerned.

Windows and doors, as well as the greater arches separating nave and choir from aisles and forming an "arcade," were of a pointed form during the Early English period, so acutely pointed indeed, sometimes, that the windows were often called "lancets." The piers of the arcades were reduced in diameter, and commonly consisted of a central pier surrounded by a cluster or group of shafts, as at Westminster (*see sketch*

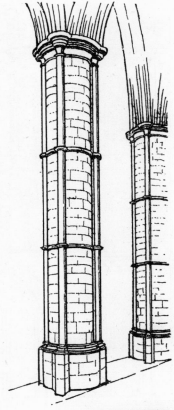

WESTMINSTER

WELLS

WESTMINSTER

117

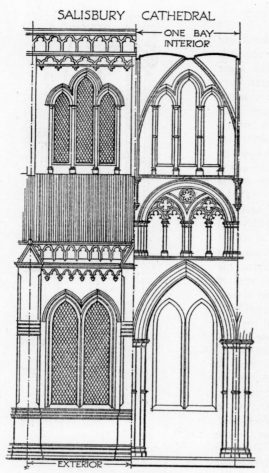

SALISBURY CATHEDRAL

ONE BAY INTERIOR

EXTERIOR

on page 117) and Salisbury. These shafts were usually of Purbeck marble, and were often connected at intervals to the central stone pier by stone annulets (*as sketch*) or by metal bands. The capitals crowning these columns generally assumed one of two forms, an inverted bell deeply moulded, or an inverted bell carved into stiff and conventional but extremely graceful foliage (*as in the sketch from Wells on page* 117). From the capitals of the arcade-piers rise the great arches, which are richly moulded with alternating rolls and hollows, thus lightening the appearance of the arch. Some of the mouldings are enriched with rows of a small ornament resembling a sharply pointed leaf or flower and commonly called the " dog-tooth " ornament. The flat spaces (" spandrils ") between the arches at Westminster are covered with a diaper pattern (*see sketch on page* 117). In fact, throughout the building, there is a tendency to increased lightness and grace, enhanced by the stained glass that now begins to appear in windows. The vaulting becomes a series of sheets made up of small stones, supported on stone ribs which spring from lofty shafts rising between the windows (*see diagram of Salisbury*). Instead of thick walls resisting the outward thrust of the vaulting by mere bulk, buttresses are placed between the windows, one opposite each pier on which the vaulting is concentrated. Thus the intermediate wall could be reduced in thickness, and windows could be increased in size and number. There were buttresses in Norman architecture, but they projected from the wall so slightly that they increased its strength very little. The diagram of Salisbury shows lancet windows in groups or clusters, three in the upper part of the wall, above the aisle roof, and two below it. It will be noticed that the interior of this cathedral is divided into three storeys or stages, and that the middle stage (the " triforium ") is hidden on the exterior by the aisle roof. This division into stages is explained on p. 120. The triforium at Salisbury helps one to understand the origin of window tracery, described on the next page.

EXAMPLES: Salisbury, 1220–66, the typical cathedral of the Early English period (*see diagram*) ; Hereford Lady Chapel, *c.* 1220 ; Southwark choir ; Brecon choir and transepts ; Wells, 1174–1242, including the wonderful west front ; Worcester choir and Lady Chapel, begun in 1224 ; and Westminster choir and transepts, 1245–60 (though this is in a transitional style between Early English and Decorated work, and is considered by some critics to be strongly French in character, with its great height and its flying buttresses).

DECORATED GOTHIC
(*c.* 1250–1300)

SOMETIMES KNOWN as Mid-Gothic,
or Middle Pointed, this style is clumsily
named " Decorated " on account of the
richness and profusion of its ornament, but
in that respect it hardly surpasses many works
of the later or " Perpendicular " period described in the next section (e.g. Henry the
Seventh's Chapel at Westminster). Critics of
fifty years ago were too prone to judge Gothic
architecture by its ornament alone, and this is
a wrong standard to apply to any form of
building, which depends primarily on its con-
structional framework or skeleton, i.e. on its
system of vaulting and buttressing. But
undoubtedly the most striking feature of this
Mid-Gothic period is the development of
the traceried window. The introduction of
stained glass and its progress from clear
greenish tints to brighter and stronger colours
made it necessary to increase the size of windows in order to light the interior of the
church adequately. Before the middle of the
thirteenth century, it became customary to
enclose a group of lancet windows under one
arch, and then to pierce the stone above the
lancets with one or more circular openings,
often in the form of a cinque-foil or quatre-
foil (*see sketch*). The arcade of the triforium at Salisbury (*see diagram on page* 118),
though not glazed, is an early example of
arches and circles grouped under an en-
closing arch. The triforium of Westminster furnishes another example of this. From
this point it was an easy transition to replace the piers between the separate lancets or
" lights " by slender shafts, and next to convert the shafts into light stone bars or
mullions. If the mullion had been square in section, it would have obstructed much of
the light. It was therefore tapered inwards and outwards from the glass, and the same
bar of stone was continued round the geometrical forms (generally circles) that filled
the upper part of the whole window.

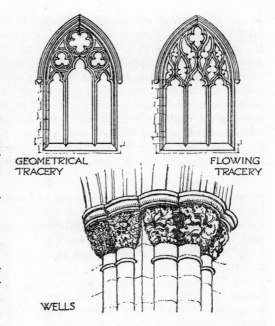

GEOMETRICAL TRACERY

FLOWING TRACERY

WELLS

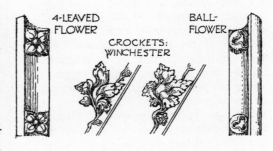

4-LEAVED FLOWER

CROCKETS: WINCHESTER

BALL-FLOWER

Thus from " plate-tracery " (i.e. lights pierced in a stone wall) was evolved " bar-tracery "
(i.e. lights separated by moulded bars of one continuous section, forming mullions in the lower
part of the window and tracery in the upper part). The next step was from geometrical
forms to more easy and flowing curves, resulting in flowing or, as it is commonly called,
" curvilinear " tracery (*see sketch*). Exeter furnishes an excellent example of tracery which
is intermediate between the geometrical and curvilinear types. The diagram illustrates this
point ; it also gives some indication of the development of the vaulting, which is broken up
into small sections by moulded ribs which resemble more and more the branches of a tree,

so that sentimental writers may be pardoned for seeing in the soaring lines of a great Mid-Gothic vault the spirit of the forest. Still more is this effect enhanced by the character of the ornament of the same period, which, instead of being conventional or stiff as hitherto, is now naturalistic in appearance, copied, some think, by the carver from actual leaves hung beside him as he worked. The capitals from Wells (*see sketch*) are typical of such foliage, and should be compared with the sketch of Early English capitals from the same cathedral. Similar naturalistic carving is to be found in all cathedrals of this period, particularly in the bosses of the vaulting, in capitals of columns and piers, and in the rich canopied tombs, niches, and other ornamental features that now are found in the larger churches. On the other hand, the "ball-flower" and the "four-leaved flower" (*see sketches on page* 119), though very characteristic of this style, are of conventional type.

The diagram of Exeter Cathedral, with those of Salisbury and Winchester, has been prepared to show the distinctive features of Gothic architecture as simply as possible. It will be noticed that the chief lighting of the church comes from the row of windows at the top, known for this reason as the "clerestory" (clear storey). Beneath this is a wide space of

wall covering the space occupied externally by the sloping roof of the aisle, and known as the triforium (or "blind storey,") because it must be dark, and cannot be lit by windows. It is, however, boldly treated with arches. The lowest stage is, of course, formed by the main arcade, or range of arches supporting the weight of the main wall and roof. Externally, each "bay" or division of the arcade is marked by a bold buttress capped by a pinnacle, which, though ornamental in appearance, has work to do. The parapet is battlemented like a castle, but it serves no military purpose. Battlemented parapets are so familiar that we are apt to forget that they are absurd. In the Perpendicular period the triforium was of little importance.

EXAMPLES : Exeter nave and choir, various dates ; Bristol choir, 1298–1332 ; Chester choir, *c.* 1283 ; St. David's Lady-Chapel, 1296–1328 ; Salisbury tower and spire, chapter-house, and cloister ; Worcester, most of nave ; Westminster, most of cloister, 1330–52 ; and Wells, chapter-house, 1293–1319, Lady-Chapel, finished 1326, and reconstruction of choir, 1329–63 [Where dates are not given above, they are uncertain, or the work was spread over various stages at different dates.]

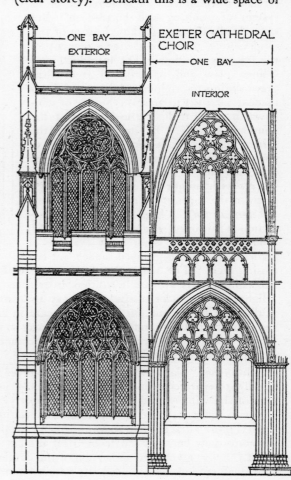

ONE BAY
EXTERIOR

EXETER CATHEDRAL CHOIR

ONE BAY

INTERIOR

PERPENDICULAR GOTHIC (*c.* 1350–*c.* 1550)

THE STYLE which has long borne this name is perhaps better described as "Rectilinear" or "Late" Gothic, for Early English architecture, as may be seen from examples illustrated in this book, abounds in strong vertical lines. On entering Salisbury or Westminster one's eye is instinctively attracted upwards. In fact, the most decided change that came into window-design after the Decorated period was the introduction of the transome, a *horizontal* stone bar, required to strengthen the mullions of the very large windows that were now becoming popular, and corresponding in section to the mullions and other bars forming the tracery. The need for transomes was caused by the rapid development of stained glass. Hitherto the glass-painters had been content to utilise such shapes as the tracery formed, the glass being secondary in importance to the tracery. But now they became more ambitious, desiring that each window should tell its story, and objecting to every stone bar that interrupted a clear field for their brush. Obviously curvilinear tracery was not to their liking, so we find that, while the size of the window was progressively enlarged, thus providing an increased surface for the artist to work on, the curved members in the tracery were gradually eliminated, until many of the windows came to resemble a gridiron.

Next, this "rectilinear" tracery was imitated in low relief on blank wall surfaces (*see diagram of Winchester*), and also in battlements and parapets. Vaulting increased in complexity, and finally reached its climax in wonderful fan-vaults (e.g. at Henry the Seventh's Chapel at Westminster, Gloucester cloisters, and the great staircase adjoining the Cathedral at Oxford). Foliage tended to become conventional again, the crockets from Winchester (*see sketches*) being typical. Among new forms of ornament that are sure indications of this period may be mentioned the "Tudor flower" (*see sketch on page* 122), and the portcullis and rose that were the emblems of the House of Tudor.

The ordinary pointed arch continued in use, but two new arch-forms were added : the "ogee," which has a double curve (*see sketch on page* 122) and was also used in the Decorated period ; and the four-centred arch, so called because it is drawn from four centres (not from two, like the pointed arch). The latter is also known as the

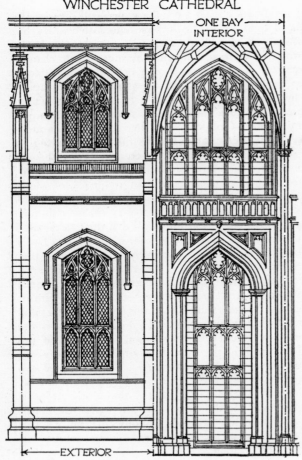

WINCHESTER CATHEDRAL

ONE BAY
INTERIOR

EXTERIOR

MANCHESTER

OGEE ARCH

TUDOR ARCH

WESTMINSTER

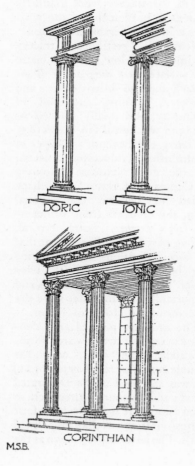

DORIC

IONIC

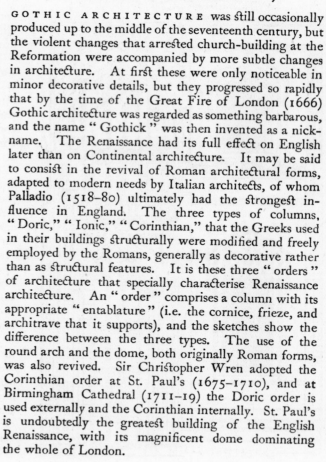

CORINTHIAN

M.S.B.

"Tudor arch" and is characteristic of late Gothic buildings (*see sketch*).

EXAMPLES: Most of St. Mary Redcliffe (Bristol); Bath Abbey, 1500–39; Chester nave; Gloucester central tower, begun 1457, Lady Chapel and cloister, 1381–1412; Manchester choir and chapterhouse 1422–58, nave 1465–81; Hereford central tower, begun 1457; Henry the Seventh's Chapel at Westminster, 1500–12; and the casing on Norman work of Winchester (1394–1460) and Gloucester.

RENAISSANCE
(17TH AND 18TH CENTURIES)

GOTHIC ARCHITECTURE was still occasionally produced up to the middle of the seventeenth century, but the violent changes that arrested church-building at the Reformation were accompanied by more subtle changes in architecture. At first these were only noticeable in minor decorative details, but they progressed so rapidly that by the time of the Great Fire of London (1666) Gothic architecture was regarded as something barbarous, and the name "Gothick" was then invented as a nickname. The Renaissance had its full effect on English later than on Continental architecture. It may be said to consist in the revival of Roman architectural forms, adapted to modern needs by Italian architects, of whom Palladio (1518–80) ultimately had the strongest influence in England. The three types of columns, "Doric," "Ionic," "Corinthian," that the Greeks used in their buildings structurally were modified and freely employed by the Romans, generally as decorative rather than as structural features. It is these three "orders" of architecture that specially characterise Renaissance architecture. An "order" comprises a column with its appropriate "entablature" (i.e. the cornice, frieze, and architrave that it supports), and the sketches show the difference between the three types. The use of the round arch and the dome, both originally Roman forms, was also revived. Sir Christopher Wren adopted the Corinthian order at St. Paul's (1675–1710), and at Birmingham Cathedral (1711–19) the Doric order is used externally and the Corinthian internally. St. Paul's is undoubtedly the greatest building of the English Renaissance, with its magnificent dome dominating the whole of London.

THIS BOOK, published by the GREAT WESTERN RAILWAY COMPANY, Paddington, London, has been printed by SPOTTISWOODE, BALLANTYNE AND COMPANY, LTD., One New-street Square, London, E.C., under the typographical direction of WILLIAM GORDON TUCKER working in co-operation with the responsible officials of the GREAT WESTERN RAILWAY. The photographs (excepting 14) were taken by the Great Western Railway Company's staff photographers, and the Pen-and-Ink Drawings are by WILLIAM M. HENDY. The Architectural Section is by MARTIN S. BRIGGS, F.R.I.B.A.